RMS TITANIC

A 21st century update to set the record straight

by

Dr Noel Stimson

Published by Dr Noel Stimson
Bembridge Isle of Wight

Cover illustration of RMS *Titanic* drawn by Gregg Berintan-Richards

ISBN: 978-1-9996923-0-8

Typeset by Desktop Studio, St Helens, Isle of Wight PO331YB

CONTENTS

This book is dedicated to the 1502 people
who died in the Titanic disaster,
their families and their descendants

Internationally known *Titanic* expert and author, David G Brown starts his 2001 book "*The Last Log of the Titanic*" with

> ***"Titanic ran over the iceberg because the berg was in its path. It sank because its hull filled with water. These are the two certainties of the tragedy."***

ILLUSTRATIONS

(Photos and images are credited where appropriate, but some are sourced from the Internet and therefore regarded as "in the public domain")

INTRODUCTION

I have often heard it said "She sailed on her maiden voyage to New York, she hit an iceberg and she sank. Get used to it!"

Amazingly, over a hundred years later, people have not got used to it! The tragic story persists and people still want to hear about it. Dozens of books and several films of the sinking have been made and as a presenter of the *Titanic* story for over 20 years I have never addressed an empty hall! I am sure other *Titanic* presenters would say the same.

Of the many books written about *Titanic*, some are factual and others somewhat fanciful, blaming anything but the iceberg for the disaster; the captain, the builders, the owners, a coal bunker fire, a missing key, even the Marconi radio operators, all come in for some level of causation or blame. Conspiracy theories and myths abound, describing the disaster as either an example of feckless pro-British greed, or an insurance scam involving switching *Titanic* for her damaged sister ship, *Olympic*. But even the best factual books are based on the 'official' version of the disaster, emanating from the two inquiries and the many press reports. I have the distinct impression that some of them may not stand up to today's scrutiny, so I decided to investigate further.

That is the *raison d'etre* for this book.

This resulted in my discovering three possible truths; the familiar story as we know it from the books and films; the rather different story as told by advocates of the conspiracy theory; and the possibility that the familiar story omitted some valuable facts that may have exposed a number of failings of some individuals, companies and government organizations involved.

As you will read, one of the major cover-ups involved Captain Smith himself. He became the perfect scapegoat as he was legally and technically responsible for the disaster as the Captain, but also conveniently dead and therefore unable to argue about being to blame. Other cover-ups have become apparent, including the general view among commentators at the time that the Inquiry Boards had pre-determined the outcomes before they even sat down.

I believe that most of the true story is hidden within the pages of the Inquiries' transcripts, in spite of several serious omissions. For this reason I have totally ignored the press and media versions of what happened, since information and evidence given under oath is more reliable than 'creative' information used to increase the sales of the newspapers.

An interesting feature about the Inquiries is the almost fanatical detail required by the questioners. For example, it would be interesting to know how the age and country of birth of the Board of Trade Inspector who signed-off the *Titanic* had any bearing on the sinking of the ship. But that is exactly what the US Inquiry Chairman, Senator William Alden Smith, asked 2nd Officer Lightoller as one of his questions on the first day, and is just one of dozens of examples of his style of pointless and time-wasting questioning. Perhaps it can only be explained as his need to cover up his total inadequacy as a maritime expert by asking as many questions as humanly possible in the hope of getting an answer that he could eventually understand.

People often ask how I became interested in the story; while enjoying supper with our friends John and Heather Board, the subject of *Titanic* cropped up in the general conversation. I have no recollection of how or why this occurred. John is a retired Master Mariner with many years at sea in the Merchant Navy; so when he told me that it was not the *Titanic* that sank, but her sister ship, RMS *Olympic*, I was astonished and allowed my incredulity to show. John said "I have a book about it. Would you like to borrow it?" I said yes, I would. The book was Robin Gardiner's book "*Titanic*

- the ship that never sank?" I was fascinated by the story as it unfolded, leading to White Star's alleged insurance scam of switching the two ships so that the badly damaged *Olympic* could be scuttled and the insurance claimed.

The 300-page book is very skillfully written by telling the usual and accepted version of the disaster with remarkable detail and accuracy, but many passages are 'seeded' with bits of the insurance scam story, giving them the false mantle of authenticity. One of the more outrageous examples is the photograph of *Olympic* at Harland & Wolff (Fig 21) showing some of the outward features of both *Titanic* and *Olympic* which Gardiner dates as 1911 in is book and showing "a vessel being re-converted from *Titanic* layout to that of *Olympic*. There can be no legitimate reason for such a conversion in 1912". As explained later, the truth is that the photo was of *Olympic*, taken not in 1911, but 9 years later in 1920, when she was being refitted back to passenger service after her service as a troopship ship in WW1.

At first, it seemed almost possible to believe this conspiracy theory, but as I read on and more and more implausible ideas were revealed, I realised that this version of the story simply was not true. But by now I was intrigued by the whole *Titanic* story and started to do some serious research. New light had been shone on the story later on, with the discovery of the wreck by Dr Robert Ballard in 1985, followed by the discovery of two pieces of the ship's bottom by divers Richie Kohler and John Chatterton in 2003.

CHAPTER 1
THE "UNSINKABLE" TITANIC

While this book is primarily about the disastrous sinking of RMS *Titanic* on her maiden voyage in April 1912, it is important that the reader has a clear understanding of the ship herself, her size, her main features, equipment and construction, and her officers and crew. All these factors had some bearing on what happened and how it all went wrong. Let's be clear about one thing before we start; there is no such thing as an unsinkable ship. However, the advertising for *Titanic* (and presumably *Olympic*) described her as "virtually unsinkable", an allusion to her 15 watertight bulkheads and double bottom, effectively making her out to be "her own lifeboat" (Fig 31). However, the press latched on to the phrase "virtually unsinkable" and then promptly dropped the first word, hence the public's view of her as unsinkable.

At 882.75 feet with a Displacement Tonnage of 52,310 tons, a Gross Registered Tonnage (GRT) of 46,000 tons, RMS *Titanic* was the largest man-made floating object in the world during her short life. She was 243 GRT tons heavier by displacement than her slightly older but closely similar sister RMS *Olympic*. (see footnote). The *Olympic* Class of ships, as they were named, were conceived in 1907 by J Bruce Ismay (Chairman of White Star) and Lord William Pirrie, managing director of Harland & Wolff (H&W), and were intended to be the largest and most luxurious liners ever. Compared to the Cunarders - White Star's main competitors in the north Atlantic - they were a massive 8,250 tons of displacement heavier and over 100 feet longer than the *Mauretania* and the *Lusitania*.

Titanic, like her sister *Olympic*, was designated as "RMS *Titanic*" as opposed to the more common "SS *Titanic*". The designation RMS *stood* for "Royal Mail Steamer", because these White Star ships had a contract with the British Royal Mail. The contract was a tough one but White Star was paid well for the service. However, there were certain stipulations about punctuality which, as you will read, had an effect on *Titanic's* speed during the crossing. Officers who worked on Royal Mail Ships would not described themselves as just Merchant Navy officers, but would proudly declare "I am a Mail Ship Officer".

There were to be three ships built to the same design and plans, *Olympic, Titanic* and *Britannic*. As we know, *Titanic* sank in 1912 after hitting an iceberg; *Britannic*, serving as a WW1 hospital ship, sank off the coast of Greece in the Kea Channel on passage to Gallipoli in 1916 after striking a mine laid by a U-Boat; she never sailed as a passenger vessel. *Olympic* also served in WW1 as a troop ship, but was the only one of the class to enjoy a long and useful career as a passenger liner, eventually being scrapped in 1937 by her new owners, Cunard.

Titanic and her sisters were built at ship builders Harland & Wolff in Belfast, who had been building White Star's ships for many years. Built almost entirely of iron and steel, she had 9 decks, a full-length double bottom and 15 watertight bulkheads. She had 4 funnels although funnel No.4 was a 'dummy', used for ventilation of the machinery spaces and the galleys only so never emitted any smoke from engine or boiler room combustion.

***Footnote**: There are various uses of the term "tonnage" when describing ships. For simplicity we are only considering two methods here. 'Displacement' is self-explanatory and refers to the ship's actual weight and the amount of water she displaces when fully loaded and floating 'on her marks' at normal draught. Gross Registered Tonnage (GRT) refers to the amount of income-earning passenger and cargo space available and does not relate to the ship's weight or mass. In GRT, 1 gross ton is equivalent to 100 cubic feet of space.*

Titanic was powered by two triple-expansion reciprocating steam engines weighing 1,000 tons each, each developing 50,000 hp at 75 revolutions, driving twin 'wing' propellers, with a centre line steam turbine engine driving a third central propeller. This turbine power unit was powered rather ingeniously by exhaust steam from the main engines. The 29 boilers were fitted with 159 coal-fired furnaces. At full speed she consumed over 800 tons of coal per day.

Titanic was equipped with 20 lifeboats although 64 were originally planned. The reasons for this are discussed in Chapter 8. There were sufficient lifejackets on board for 3,500 people. There was a telephone system throughout the ship, including the crow's nest, with loudspeakers on the bridge.

Communication with the outside world was provided by the Marconi Wireless Company. The two Marconi operators, Jack Phillips and Harold Bride were often incorrectly regarded as ship's officers; employed by Marconi, they also drew pay from White Star. Their radio equipment had a range of 250 miles in daytime and 1500 miles at night. There was no regulation requiring them to do so (this came later after the disaster), but Phillips and Bride kept a 24-hour watch between them. Many other ships had only one Marconi operator, making a 24-hour watch impractical. Their primary function, however, was to make money for the Marconi company by sending messages ashore for the wealthier passengers, who liked to indulge themselves in this relatively new technology. Operating a communications service regarding the navigation of the ship, such as receiving warnings of ice, was very much a secondary consideration and probably accounts for the operators' rather casual attitude in not sending certain important messages immediately to the bridge (see Chapter 3). This drew considerable criticism from the Inquiry Boards at the time as well as from our own 21st century safety-conscious viewpoint. But it is important to remember these events took place over 100 years ago.

Being the largest ships in the world caused its own problems. Their sheer size meant that there were few captains capable or experienced enough to handle them. In general, things went impressively well, but there were incidents such as *Titanic's* departure from Southampton when a touch too much power from *Titanic's* wash caused the nearby SS *New York* to be wrenched away from the dock, with almost catastrophic results.

The passenger accommodation for first class passengers was staggeringly luxurious, equivalent to anything seen in the most expensive Mayfair hotels or clubs. Apart from delightful cabins and staterooms, first class passengers had access to a swimming pool, a gymnasium, squash courts, top class restaurants and a 'Cafe Parisienne'. Second and third class passengers had less glamorous surroundings, though for many, still much grander than they might have been accustomed to.

While the two ships were supposed to be identical twins, built at the same yard and from the same set of blue prints and plans, there were a huge number of detail differences due to issues that cropped up on the *Olympic* - the prototype for the class – which needed to be addressed in *Titanic*. Some of the more significant differences are discussed in Chapter 5. Major changes in the layout of the accommodations meant that even crew transferred from *Olympic* to *Titanic* had difficulty finding their way round.

One thing was clear; the passengers and crew were not allowed to mix, and the layout made sure that this was so. While passengers enjoyed themselves aboard in so many ways, on the other side of the rich oak and mahogany panelling, crewmen in greasy overalls would be beavering away at their work. However, this rule was relaxed for the officers, who were allowed to mix socially with the passengers when they were off duty. Some officers, such as the ship's Purser, Doctor and Marconi operators, would speak with passengers frequently in the course of their work.

As most people understand, there were not enough lifeboats on *Titanic* for all the passengers and crew (Chapter 8). The British Board of Trade

(BoT) regulations of the day required only 16 lifeboats for any vessel over 10,000 tons, so the 20 lifeboats with which *Titanic* was equipped actually exceeded the regulatory requirements by having 4 extra 'Engelhardt' collapsible lifeboats, A, B, C and D, positioned just behind and on the roof of the bridge and chartroom.

The 20 boats together could have saved almost 1200 people out of the 2,206 on board, or of the 3,400 she could have had if the maiden voyage had been fully booked. In the event only 706 were rescued from the lifeboats. When this was announced, everyone was deeply shocked, and especially today, people cannot believe that any ship would set sail with lifeboat places for only one third of its possible complement. To make sense of this and to get it into the context of the early 20th century, we need to look at the approach to lifeboats at that time.

To begin with, *Titanic* was not the only passenger liner with insufficient lifeboats; *Olympic* was the same, as were all the other White Star ships, the Cunard ships, and just about every other major shipping line travelling the oceans with vessels of similar size. It was a normal state of affairs at that time.

The situation had come about by the Board of Trade Regulations regarding lifeboats being somewhat out of date and failing to keep up with the increasing size and complexity in current ship design. Yet the wider truth meant that the BoT Regulations in the early 20th century required a passenger ship to provide a lifeboat place for all on board, unless a ship had sufficient watertight compartments to render it effectively 'her own lifeboat' just as the *Olympic* Class ships were heralded; in which case the '16 lifeboats' rule applied as a concession. *Olympic* and *Titanic* were each around 46,000 tons GRT, and were actually fitted with 20 lifeboats, 4 more than required by the regulations. Ship owners and builders at that time were caught between out-of-date regulations and the need to minimize costs.

Titanic's Board of Trade Inspector's report stated:

> *"I was on board this ship immediately before she sailed (from Southampton). I saw two boats swung out and lowered into the water. From the foregoing reports of inspection, and from what I saw myself, I was satisfied that the ship was in all respects fit for the intended voyage, and that the requirements under the Merchant Shipping Acts have been complied with."*

Captain Maurice Clarke, BoT Inspector; 3 April 1912.

(Note: this is not the same Captain (Arthur) Clarke that sat on the London Board of Inquiry; the latter was representing Trinity House, not the Board of Trade.)

However, at the US Senate Inquiry, 2nd Officer Charles Lightoller gave a slightly contradictory version of the event:

(Senator Smith) *Tell just what was done.*
(2nd Officer Lightoller). *All the boats on the ship were swung out and those that I required were lowered down as far as I wanted them - some all the way down, and some (6) dropped into the water.*

US Senate Inquiry Day 1

Apparently, this was sufficient according to the regulations of the day, but does not explain how many of the crew were involved in the tests or how well they carried out their duties. Not only were *Titanic's* crew in general unfamiliar with the lifeboats and how to launch them, but none of the 60 seamen on board seem to know if they had been allocated a lifeboat station. A lifeboat roster had been prepared and posted but It seems few of the crew were aware of it.

(Commissioner) *"What I want to know is whether you had any (lifeboat) station to which you were to go?*
(Quartermaster Robert Hichens) *"Not that I am aware of, no."*

London Inquiry Day 8

It is interesting to note that today all ships are required to not only provide at least one seat in a lifeboat per person on board on each side of the ship, but also that all seaman crew must hold a 'lifeboat certificate' qualifying them to handle every type of ship's boat carried on that vessel. They are also allocated a lifeboat to crew. Another factor was the attitude towards such matters in those days. Like the parachute, the crash helmet or seat belt, they were all ideas whose time had not yet come. Lifeboats were regarded more as extra ships' boats, useful items of equipment for moving crew, passengers, stores or equipment from ship to shore. In a rescue situation they could also be used for transferring passengers to rescue vessels in a sort of shuttle service. The idea that an entire ship's complement of passengers and crew might one day need a full set of lifeboats in an emergency was never entertained by the owners. The 20 boats provided were little more than a gesture to the regulations. 64 boats were in the original plans of the 1908 specification for the *Olympic* class ships, but the number was whittled down to 20 over the build period due to pressures of cost and space. *Titanic* in particular was being advertised as "virtually unsinkable" and Ismay believed that too many lifeboats on show would send the wrong message as well as take up too much boat deck space, limiting the First Class passengers' ability to promenade!

The original number of 64 planned boats sounds huge, but Harland & Wolff had commissioned a new design of lifeboat davit from the Welin company; each pair of davits was designed to hold up to 4 lifeboats on a new 'track and stack' system, but in the end there was only one boat fitted to each pair, which rendered Welin's brilliant, expensive and innovative design utterly pointless.

It is interesting to note that when *Olympic* arrived in New York two weeks after the sinking, she was carrying 42 lifeboats! They were said to be a motley bunch of scruffy boats, gathered up at short notice from nearby laid-up ships and shipyards at Southampton. But at least there was a seat in a lifeboat for every passenger on that particular voyage.

Titanic's sea trials took place on April 2nd 1912. They lasted approximately 10 hours and consisted of *Titanic* working up to about 85% of maximum speed and checking how she handled during various manoeuvers such as straight ahead, turning to port, turning to starboard and a crash stop using full power astern. Her tightest turning circle at 20 knots was 1.9 nautical miles (2.2 statute miles) in diameter (Fig 32), and she could do a crash-stop in 850 yards – less than half a mile and equal to less than 3 ship's lengths. These figures will be useful later on when the actual collision itself is considered.

The ship's senior officers, Chief Officer Henry Wilde, 1st Officer William Murdoch, 2nd Officer Charles Lightoller and the junior officers, Joseph Boxhall, Harold Lowe and Herbert Pitman had all travelled up by train from Southampton to Liverpool and then took the ferry across to Belfast. Captain Edward J Smith arrived two days later and relieved Captain Herbert Haddock who had been running the earlier trials.

After the sea trials where finished, *Titanic* returned to the fitting out wharf to disembark the sea trials crew and BoT officials, and effect the official handover to White Star. She picked up a few lately-arrived stores, and proceeded immediately to Southampton with her 150 delivery crew. The rush was on to get the maiden voyage under way on time, especially as it was already three weeks late.

The delivery crew, almost to a man, returned to Belfast by train after the ship had arrived at Southampton. This was perfectly normal as the crew were mostly Belfast men. The new crew for the maiden voyage joined the ship at Southampton, White Star's main sea-going base, and where they mostly lived, including Captain Smith.

Of course, those who follow the conspiracy theory believe the delivery crew quit the ship at Southampton because they knew something was wrong. We will leave that one to the reader.

CHAPTER 2
WHAT HAPPENED

A summary of the official version based on the inquiries

On Wednesday 10 April 1912, at 12 noon *Titanic* sailed from Southampton on her maiden voyage across the Atlantic to New York, via Cherbourg and Queenstown. The ship had just days before, been signed off by the Board of Trade Inspector, Captain Maurice Clarke.

Titanic was carrying 2206 souls, including a ship's company of 876. She called in first at Cherbourg and then Queenstown (now Cobh, the port for Cork in the Republic of Ireland) to pick up more passengers and mail, first and second class passengers from Cherbourg, and mainly migrants (steerage class) from Ireland.

Approximately 1,000 miles from her destination New York on Sunday 14th April she struck an iceberg at 11:40 pm ship's time. She sank 2hrs and 40 minutes later. 705 people were saved in the inadequate number of half-filled lifeboats, and over 1500 lives were lost, including the Captain, Edward John Smith, and three of his most senior officers, Chief Engineer Joseph Bell, Chief Officer Henry Wilde and 1st Officer William Murdoch, Thomas Andrews, the ship's designer, and the 6 members of the Guarantee Party. All 35 engineer officers and the ship's seven-piece orchestra also perished.

Several ships picked up *Titanic's* distress calls but only the SS *Carpathia* (Fig 27) was close enough to dash to the rescue, at 58 miles away. This she did magnificently, the 14-knot vessel reaching almost 18 knots. She arrived at dawn, about 04:30, and picked up the 705 survivors from lifeboats, just over 2 hours after the ship and 1500 people had sunk below the surface of the Atlantic.

Two inquiries were held shortly after the disaster (Chapter 11); after 4 days a US Senate sub-committee met in the Waldorf Hotel in New York and a week later moved to Washington, all for a total of 18 days. It was chaired by Senator William Walden Smith (no relation to Captain Smith). However, the Inquiry members' lack of understanding or experience of maritime matters became embarrassingly obvious from Day 1.

Two weeks later, the British inquiry, under the orders of the Board of Trade and chaired by the Commissioner for Wrecks Sir Charles Bigham, Lord Mersey, was held at the London Scottish Drill Hall, Buckingham Gate in London. It lasted for 36 days. Both inquiries came to broadly similar conclusions and made similar recommendations to improve safety at sea. However, there was a degree of competitiveness as to which Inquiry might be seen as the more thorough, which may have accounted for the rather pompous, repetitious and often pointless and penetrating nature of the questioning at both inquiries.

Fig 1. *Titanic* leaving H&W for sea trials in Belfast Loch. 2nd April 1912 (Robin Gardiner)

Fig 2. Marconi operators Jack Phillips and . . . Harold Bride (Robin Gardiner)

Fig 3. *Titanic's* crow's nest and . . . Lookout Fred Fleet

(Walter Lord)

Fig 4. *Olympic's* officers 1911. Captain Smith (centre) with Chief Officer Evans (L) and 1st Officer Murdoch (R) with 2nd Officer Lightoller (Back row L) (Granger Collection)

Fig 5. Captain Smith with Purser McElroy (W Lord)

Fig 6. White Star Managing Director J Bruce Ismay (R Gardiner)

Fig 7. Chief Officer Henry Wilde *Titanic's* second in command
(W Lord)

Fig 8. Thomas Andrews, managing director of Harland & Wolff and designer of the '*Olympic*' Class
(Anton Gill)

P. C. Taylor — W. T. Brailey — J. L. Hume — G. Krins — W. Woodward — W. Hartley (Leader).

MEMBERS OF THE "TITANIC'S" BAND WHO DIED AT THEIR POST

Fig 9. The ship's orchestra (W Lord)

Fig 10a. (Above L) VAD nurse Violet Jessop, (Bruce Beveridge) and

Fig 10b. (Above R) her brother, AB Frank Jessop (John Woodford)

Fig 11. (L) Lookout Robert Hichens (Enc. Titanica)

CHAPTER 3
THE ICE WARNINGS

We need to bear in mind that these were the relatively early days of the use of wireless telegraphy at sea and not every ship was fitted out with the very expensive equipment, although by 1912 the use of wireless was increasing considerably. The operators were often regarded as ship's officers but they were actually employees of, and paid by, the Marconi Company, which was under contract to supply wireless communication services to the ships. *Titanic* had two Marconi operators, Jack Philips and his assistant operator, Harold Bride.

The routines, courtesies and protocols employed in maritime communication all came from the more rudimentary days of flags and arm-waving and were in the process of being refined internationally as the use of wireless grew and developed in its own way in different countries. The system required the use of Morse Code to spell out each letter and the operators would become very skilled at reading and transmitting messages at high speeds. Confusing the issue was the fact that two systems were in operation at that time, Continental Morse and American Morse (a situation which apparently caused great difficulty for the American operators receiving the names of survivors from SS *Carpathia*). The situation was resolved at the International Radio Telegraphic Convention in 1913, in favour of the Continental system.

The International Distress call since 1904 had been 'CQ' or 'CQD' but at the International Radio Telegraphic Convention in 1905 it was changed to 'SOS' although not generally adopted internationally until 1909. However, some operators preferred the old 'CQD', which is why both protocols were in use as late as 1912.

Interestingly, SOS is not an acronym for 'Save Our Souls' as many of us learned while in the Boy Scouts etc. It was chosen because it comprised an easy-to-recognise Morse pattern -

"dit dit dit - dah dah dah - dit dit dit (... ___ ...)"

There were 6 messages warning of ice in the vicinity received by *Titanic's* Marconi operators, but the two most crucial messages never reached the bridge. The six messages were transmitted and received as follows:

09:00. SS *Caronia*: Captain Barr reported *"icebergs, growlers and field ice in 42N:49.51W. Compliments Captain Barr"*

13:42. RMS *Baltic* (Captain Smith's first White Star command) relayed message from SS *Athenai* about *"Icebergs and large quantities of ice today in 41.51N, 49.52W".* Captain Smith acknowledged the message but for some unknown reason, handed it to Ismay without at first sharing it with the bridge. Ismay read it later and subsequently showed it to some passengers, which he denied at the Inquiry. Both actions were regarded as improper by the Inquiries. However, Smith recovered the message from Ismay early in the evening and took it to the bridge to be placed on the chart room board as normal, before joining the Widener's dinner party.

13:45. SS *Amerika*: (message to US Hydrographic Office and intercepted by *Titanic*): *"Passed two large icebergs in 41.27N, 50.08W on 14 April".*

19:30. SS *Californian* to SS *Antillian*: Intercepted by *Titanic* and read *"At 42.03N, 49.09W. Three large bergs 5 miles to the south of us. Regards, Capt Lord".* This message was delivered to the bridge.

21:40. SS *Mesaba*: "*To all eastbound ships. Ice report. In 42.41N to 41.25N, 49W to 50.03W. Heavy pack ice and great number large icebergs, also field ice.*" Philips acknowledged the message but did not confirm it had been passed to the Captain, probably because it did not contain the all-important MSG prefix (see paragraphs below). This message never got to the bridge even though it was a crucial ice warning that would most probably have caused Captain Smith to stop *Titanic* in her tracks.

23:00. SS *Californian*: *"We are stuck and surrounded by ice"*. An apparently casual message from Evans in *Californian* to Philips in *Titanic*, with no MSG prefix. The message was actually ordered by Captain Lord and should have been addressed to Captain Smith with the MSG prefix. This did not happen.

The first three messages suggested strongly to Smith that there was a clear 24 nautical mile gap in the ice dead ahead of *Titanic* (Fig 13) comfortably large enough for *Titanic's* 92 foot beam to slide though! The fourth message from *Antillian* at 19:30 simply confirmed the ice lying clear to the north of *Titanic's* track. Although Smith knew he was entering a general area of ice, what he was unaware of was the extensive field of growlers and bergs spread across the sea right in front of him, completely filling that apparent 24-mile gap, because none of the messages so far received on the bridge were reporting on that area.

As mentioned earlier, there was a convention among wireless operators that any message concerned with the navigation of the ship must have the coded prefix 'MSG' (acronym for 'Master's Special Gram') and must go straight to the Captain or the Officer of the Watch, before being signed-off by him as 'received', acknowledged to the sender and then posted on the chart room message board to be seen by all the ship's officers. This did not happen with the *Mesaba* message as the MSG prefix was omitted. Similarly, the message from *Californian* also had no MSG prefix as it was also sent directly from operator to operator. The prefix used was 'OMM' which virtually means *"I say old man, . . . "* and went on to say *"We are stopped and surrounded by ice"*.

Jack Philips was annoyed by this as *Californian's* transmissions were interfering with his own efforts to send off the many private messages from passengers, delayed and piling up on his desk due to a technical problem earlier in the day. Philips sent a stern rebuke to *Californian's* operator with *"DDD (code for 'shut up'); I am working Cape Race and you are jamming me".* *Californian's* Marconi operator switched off his equipment at 23:30 and turned in for the night, 10 minutes before *Titanic* struck the iceberg. Both the messages were placed under a paperweight on the desk. If the *Mesaba* and *Californian* operators had used the MSG prefix, those messages would have been in effect from Captain to Captain and gone straight to the bridge. Who knows how Captain Smith would have responded to that information? (Fig 14).

The two messages that would without any doubt have informed Captain Smith of the mass of ice that lay directly in his path never reached the bridge, so neither he nor his officers on the bridge had an opportunity to read them. No wonder they felt it was acceptable to keep working up the ship's speed.

At midnight, following the collision with the iceberg, Captain Smith came into the Marconi wireless office at midnight to tell the operators, Phillips and Bride, to stand by to send the distress signal CQD, "but not till I tell you" he added. Forty minutes later Smith returned with the instruction "Send CQD now". Bride chipped in with *"Maybe we should send the new SOS, sir? It could be the last chance we get!"* and they all laughed at the black humour.

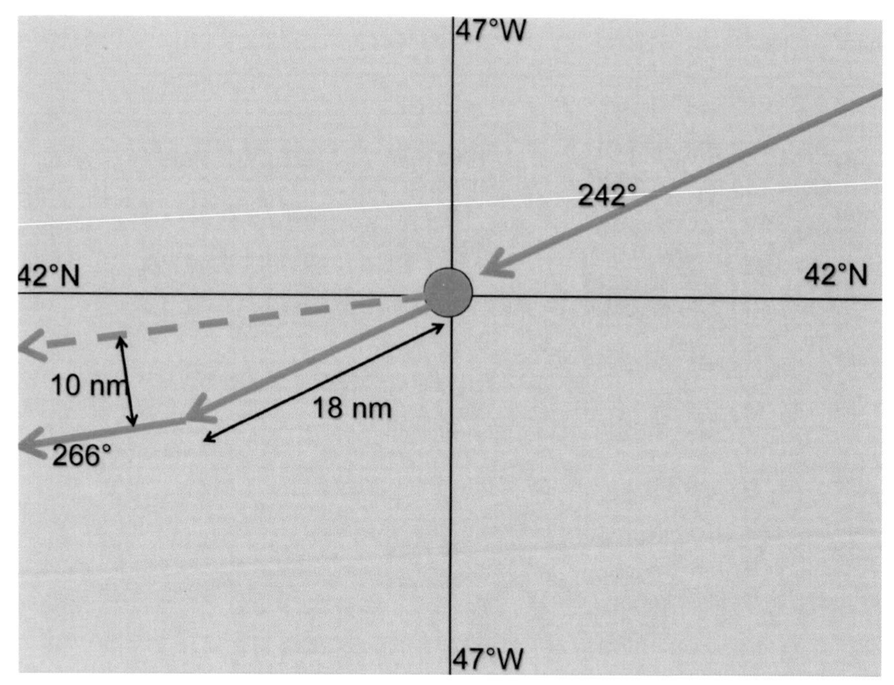

Fig 12. "The Corner" at 42N. 47W. (Author)

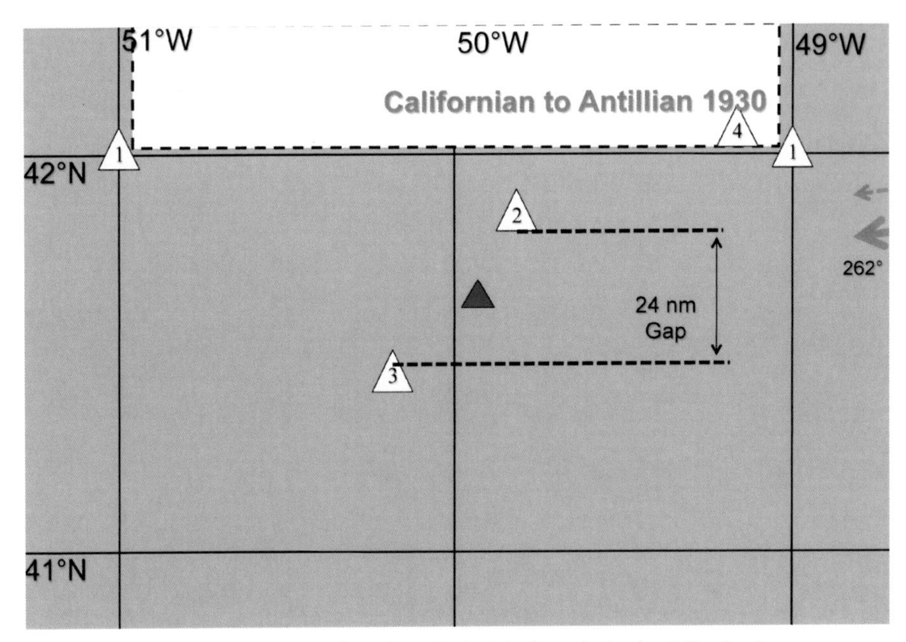

Fig 13. The 24 nm gap in the ice that Captain Smith thought he had (Author)

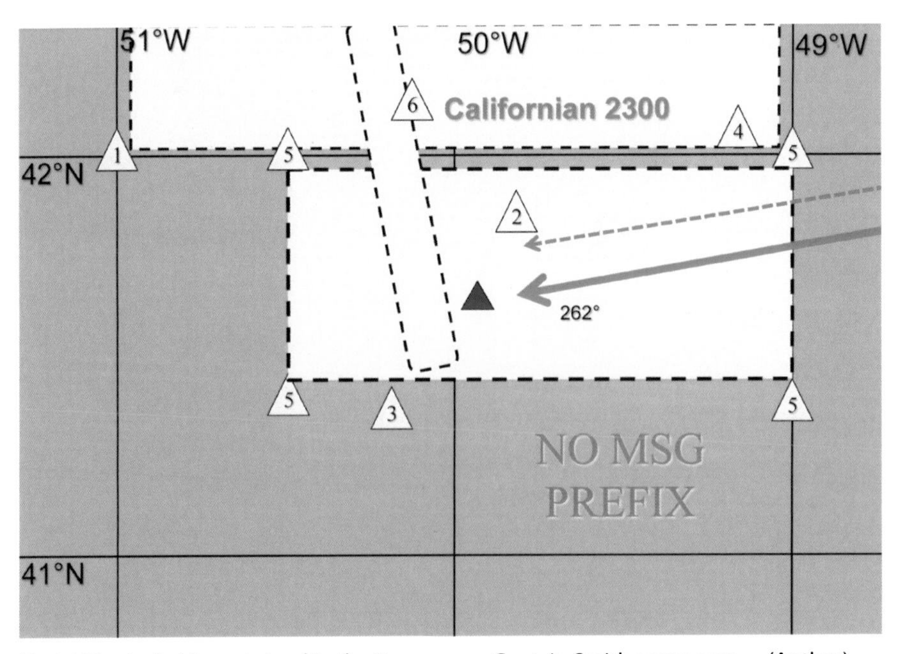

Fig 14. The icefields contained in the 2 messages Captain Smith never saw (Author)

CHAPTER 4
WHAT SOME PEOPLE BELIEVE HAPPENED – THE CONSPIRACY THEORY

Fact: On 20th September 1911, the world's largest and White Star's newest ship, RMS *Olympic* under the command of Captain E J Smith, with Trinity House pilot Captain George Bowyer on board, was leaving Southampton Water on her fifth Atlantic crossing.

Unfortunately, she was in collision with HMS *Hawke*, an 8,000-ton Royal Navy cruiser from the Victorian era off the Isle of Wight, as *Hawke* was returning to Portsmouth after speed trials in the Western Solent. It seems that as *Olympic* rounded Brambles Bank off Cowes and turned to port (left) onto her easterly heading for Spithead, she came up on a parallel course to *Hawke* which was by that time one and a half cables (300 yards) to the south. As *Olympic* slowed in her turn to port round West Brambles buoy, *Hawke*, abeam of *Olympic*, was travelling faster and effectively became the 'overtaking vessel'. She seemed to try to accelerate past but misjudged *Olympic's* own acceleration which left *Hawke* struggling to keep up. When the two ships were almost off Osborne Bay, *Olympic* was on course for the southern channel past Ryde Middle, heading down to the Nab lightship and out into the English Channel. At which point, *Hawke* inexplicably turned violently to port, apparently trying to pass under *Olympic's* stern and head into Portsmouth.

The timing of the turn appeared to the observers to have been badly misjudged and *Hawke's* ram bow slammed into *Olympic* 90 feet from her stern, punching two large holes in her hull, one above and one below the waterline. Fortunately there were no casualties on either vessel.

The reality was that as *Olympic*, under the advice of Trinity House Pilot Captain George Bowyer, turned to port to follow the narrow shipping lane, HMS *Hawke's* captain, Cdr William Blunt RN, gave the order to turn to starboard to keep clear of *Olympic*. The helm order was something like "port 15" (in accordance with the convention of that time, when helm orders were given as tiller orders, which then turned the rudder and the ship the other way). The cruiser started to turn to starboard as ordered, but then turned suddenly and violently swung to port, and it instantly appeared, from Cdr Blunt's explosive reaction, that the hapless quartermaster, PO Reginald Hunt, had turned the ship's wheel the wrong way! Cdr Blunt then called for an urgent correction, but Hunt yelled back "I didn't, sir, but the helm is jammed!". Blunt ordered full astern on both engines as 3 sailors tried to help Hunt turn the jammed wheel, all to no avail and too late to avoid the impact. In spite of the quartermaster turning the wheel correctly, it seems it was *Olympic's* propeller wash that had sucked *Hawke* into the collision. The 8,000-ton bang was colossal, and according to one witness, "sounded like a howitzer going off". The *Hawke* was deeply impaled into *Olympic's* side, but as the current from *Olympic's* forward motion took effect, *Hawke* was torn away sideways and her massive concrete-reinforced steel ram-bow was wrenched off (Figs 15, 16, 17). Fortunately, *Hawke's* No. 1 watertight bulkhead held and she was able to make her way slowly but safely into Portsmouth.

Olympic went slowly back to Southampton under her own power and, after disembarking her passengers, was placed into White Star's repair facility. There the damage was assessed and patched up and two weeks later the ship limped back to Harland & Wolff in Belfast at 10 knots under one engine for permanent repairs in their main dry dock. When she arrived at H&W she was still taking on water, and was sitting so far below her marks that she needed several hundred tons of water pumped out before she was able to float over the cill and enter the dry dock.

There was the usual Admiralty Inquiry following such an incident, to which only Royal Navy personnel were allowed to attend. This meant that neither Captain Smith, Captain George Bowyer nor their legal representatives were allowed in court. The court found Smith and Bowyer jointly responsible for the collision since it was claimed that *Olympic* did not allow enough space for *Hawke* in the narrow channel and that the suction from *Olympic's* huge propulsion system had pulled *Hawke* into a collision. The commander of HMS *Hawke* was exonerated and later promoted to Captain, in spite of the well-known rule at sea that an overtaking vessel must keep clear of, and not hamper the maneuverability of the other vessel. The suction explanation would not have been an issue if Hawke had prudently kept clear of *Olympic*, which actually maintained her proper course as required when being overtaken. She was also more than 6 times the displacement of *Hawke*, yet another reason for the naval vessel to maintain a safe distance! The question of the possible jammed helm was ignored by the inquiry, as was the fact that Cdr Blunt should never have attempted an overtaking maneuver in such confined waters in the first place; it was bad seamanship, in this author's opinion, for the following reasons:

The international Regulations for the Prevention of Collisions at Sea (1972) (COLREGS) state:

Rule 9:

- *A vessel proceeding along a narrow channel must keep to starboard.*
- *Small vessels or sailing vessels must not impede (larger) vessels which can navigate only within a narrow channel.*

Rule 13:

. . . . an overtaking vessel must keep out of the way of the vessel being overtaken. "Overtaking" means approaching another vessel at more than 22.5 degrees abaft her beam. . . . Note that . . . this rule overrides all other rules.

With the assumption that the rules in 1912 were similar to today's COLREGS, these two rules would seem to make it clear that *Hawke* was to blame; she was the overtaking vessel and was expected to "keep clear". She was also smaller than *Olympic*, which was a very large vessel navigating in a narrow channel. Added to which, Rule 13 over-rides all other rules. Even if this was not the case in 1912, the hearing seems to have broken all the most basic rules of British law, starting with the age-old tenet of one being innocent until proven to be guilty! How can this be upheld if one side of the 'argument' is not allowed in the court? The Admiralty Inquiry was in general regarded as a 'stitch-up' by the Navy.

Since the unfavourable Admiralty Inquiry blamed White Star (i.e. Captain Smith and pilot Captain George Bowyer) for the accident, there would be no insurance payout to cover the repairs or the lost income from cancelled voyages, alone estimated at £250,000, and White Star would have to foot the bill. White Star refused to accept the Admiralty decision and issued a writ against Cdr Blunt. The Navy counter-sued and after a 9-day hearing, the Admiralty decision was upheld. White Star took the matter to the Appeal Court and then to the House of Lords, and lost on each occasion.

The outcome was the result of White Star's inability to convince the various courts that HMS *Hawke* was the overtaking vessel and therefore was required to keep clear of RMS *Olympic*, instead of the other way round, though it is hard to imagine how a 50,000-ton vessel could manage such a manoeuver in a confined channel. It would have been so much better for *Hawke* to have reduced speed slightly as soon as it became a close quarters situation, so she could safely slip under *Olympic's* stern.

The damage to *Olympic* was said to be extensive, though perhaps somewhat exaggerated; apart from the holes in the hull, the starboard propeller shaft was bent, and allegedly the starboard engine, which weighed 1,000 tons, was shifted off its mountings, one hull frame and a nearby keel section were bent and some say the midline propeller shaft was also bent, though this was an assumption based on the fact the midline steam turbine engine was not used on the short voyage back to Belfast. Some reckoned the damage was so extensive, possibly requiring a complete re-build of the after end of the ship, that it would be uneconomic to repair her. Others believed that repair was feasible and it seems that is what happened. Understandably, any thought of 'writing off' *Olympic* was completely unacceptable to all concerned.

In order to expedite the repairs to *Olympic*, several items ear-marked for *Titanic* were, allegedly, re-directed to *Olympic*; this definitely included part of *Titanic's* starboard propeller shaft. Inevitably this process caused delays to *Titanic's* build programme, which partly explains the pressure on White Star to get *Titanic's* maiden voyage under way in April, 3 weeks late.

So far as we know, the records all show that *Olympic* was successfully and properly repaired and back in service by the end of November 1911, but returned to the Belfast dry dock in February 1912 with a lost or damaged starboard propeller blade from hitting an unmarked submerged wreck off New York harbour entrance. Again, *Titanic's* resources were used to get Olympic back into service.

In November/December 1912, 7 months after the loss of *Titanic, Olympic* went in for a major refit; this included an updated cabin arrangement in the foc'sle so she now had *Titanic's* familiar 16-port hole arrangement on the C deck forecastle. She also had the aft B deck promenade shortened to make space for the enlarged Second Class accommodation, as in *Titanic*. In addition, her double bottom was extended up the sides to just above the waterline in the mid-ships section, 5 watertight bulkheads were extended right up to the weather decks, and, most significant of all, she was fitted with 64 lifeboats.

THE CONSPIRACY

All the above is based on the facts as we know them. However, a few years ago, suspicion was raised on the question of whether or not *Olympic* was actually repaired fully or simply patched up to play a dramatic new role.

This new conspiracy theory, created by author Robin Gardiner, claimed that the damage was so extensive and the cost so high that the White Star Board secretly hatched an ingenious plan to solve the problem. Allegedly, White Star's plan was to switch the two ships' identities, sending *Olympic* to sea disguised as *Titanic* on her maiden voyage, to run her into an ice field and scuttle her, having arranged for ships to be standing by ready to safely take off the passengers and crew. The plan would have had major financial advantages; White Star could collect on the insurance and there would be no need for expensive permanent repairs. This would mean that it was actually *Olympic* lying at the bottom of the Atlantic, and it was *Titanic* that was scrapped in 1937!

It was claimed that since the two ships were virtually identical, a swap would be a relatively simple process that should take no more than a weekend! This was made even more simple by pure chance as the two ships were almost alongside each other at the Harland & Wolff shipyard for several weeks in October/November 1911. *Olympic* was in the dry dock being repaired following the accident with *Hawke* and *Titanic* was nearing completion at the fitting out wharf a short distance away. A golden opportunity had presented itself to start switching the ships' identities, or so it would seem. (Fig 20)

In the event, the entire plan fell apart when the *Titanic/Olympic* hybrid (if that is what she was) actually struck an iceberg, and we know what happened after that.

Fig 15. Painting of the collision between
RMS *Olympic* and HMS *Hawke* on Sept 20th 1911
(Internet)

Fig 16. Collision damage to RMS *Olympic*
(similar damage below the waterline) (G C Cooper)

Fig 17. Collision damage to HMS *Hawke* showing ram bow was torn away
(G C Cooper)

Fig 18. RMS *Titanic* departing on her maiden voyage (Frank Beken)
Note partially-screened A-Deck promenade

Fig 19. RMS *Olympic* in Southampton Water en route for
Cherbourg and New York (F Beken)   Note open A-Deck promenade

Fig 20. *Olympic* (L) being warped into dry dock,
with *Titanic* (R) on the fitting out wharf 1911
(Robin Gardiner)

Fig 21. Conspiracy theorists' "1911 evidence of *Olympic* changing her identity".
Note *Olympic's* open A-deck, *Titanic's* 16 portholes on C-deck foc'sl and
shorter B-deck aft promenade (hardly visible at RH edge).
This photo was actually taken in June 1920 during HMTS *Olympic's* post-WW1 refit,
converting her back to passenger service. (UFT Museum)

CHAPTER 5
WHAT WERE THE DIFFERENCES BETWEEN TITANIC AND OLYMPIC?

The two ships were basically identical twin sisters, built from the same drawings, and a third ship, *Britannic*, was on the way to being built. However, as often happens with prototypes, there were a few problems with the brand new *Olympic*. This meant that the designers would have to make several adjustments and changes to the second ship within the layout of the accommodation. However the ships were so close to being identical that the company was able to use pictures of *Olympic* to advertise *Titanic*, and vice versa (Fig 44).

A DECK (Figs 18 and 19)

Due to complaints of spray from First Class passengers, White Star (Ismay) decided to place a steel and glass screen covering the forward half of the A-Deck promenade to solve the problem. According to some, this seems to be an over-reaction to such a minor problem, and it was thought that the screen was actually built in order to stiffen the structure of the ship as early sea trials allegedly showed that her hull was 'panting' - flexing in and out of the ship's sides when crossing waves - a worrying sign of hull weakness but one for which there is no real evidence. The reality was that *Titanic* was not panting as she was an extraordinarily strong vessel.

B DECK (Figs 18 and 19)

On *Titanic* the forward section of this deck was completely different to *Olympic*, where it was a First Class passenger promenade deck. This was changed in *Titanic* by extending the First Class cabins out to the ship's sides on the port side, making them larger and more luxurious, and installing the 'A La Carte' restaurant and the 'Café Parisienne' on the starboard side, thereby eliminating the First Class promenade on B Deck altogether. This also necessitated a change in the window arrangements which in *Titanic* were in irregular groups of two or three windows, while *Olympic's* B-Deck windows were all evenly spaced.

White Star found they needed to increase *Titanic*'s B-Deck Second Class accommodation aft, so they replaced some of the recreational spaces with cabins. This had the effect of reducing the length of the aft promenade deck by half.

C DECK FOC'SLE (Fig 22)

White Star decided to make extensive changes to the crew accommodation in the section between the forward well deck and the bow. This resulted in the need for additional portholes, so that unlike *Olympic's* evenly-spaced 14 portholes, T*itanic* had 16 with two extra portholes forming a distinctive cluster of 5 portholes close to the after end of that deck. This new improved arrangement appeared on *Olympic* following her 1912 refit and was also included in *Britannic*.

Fig 22. *Titanic's* 16-porthole arrangement;
2 extra porthole cluster at the aft end. (H&W)

BRIDGE CABS (Fig 23)

One difference that is quite difficult to spot on many photographs is the extra width of *Titanic's* bridge wings. Unlike *Olympic's* which were flush with the ship's side, *Titanic's* bridge cabs extended beyond the ship's side by about 18 inches, giving much better visibility when docking.

Fig 23. Captain Smith can be seen peering out from *Titanic's* starboard bridge cab, showing its 18-inch projection. (W Lord)

Taken at Queenstown and probably the last photo taken of Captain Smith. Note the swung-out emergency boat (Lifeboat #1) on its davits

CHAPTER 6
DE-BUNKING THE CONSPIRACY

"How could anyone expect to keep 14,000 Irish shipyard workers quiet?"
Member's question, Island Sailing Club, Cowes – talk 2012

Advocates of the conspiracy believe that the wreck is actually *Olympic* and have come up with some novel examples to 'prove' it, such as "one of the starboard propeller blades has *Titanic's* build number 401 stamped on the blade". They claim this was due to a *Titanic* 'spare' being fitted to *Olympic* in February 1912. It also suggests just as strongly that the wreck is actually *Titanic*!

THE SWITCH

Switching the two ship's identities successfully could not have been done in such a short time as a weekend! While there were a few obvious differences between them that could be easily seen from a distance away as the ship sailed past, there were literally thousands of differences to be seen only when one was on board (see Chapter 5). Anyone familiar with *Olympic* would know instantly they were on a different ship when they boarded *Titanic*.

Discussing the conspiracy theory during a presentation at the Island Sailing Club in Cowes, a member of the audience commented "How could anyone possibly expect to keep 14,000 Irish shipyard workers quiet?". This is countered by the conspiracy theorists who say that all the shipyard workers, and the ships' crews, were sworn to some kind of Official Secrets Act, but there is no hard evidence for this beyond the level of 'gossip'.

PHOTO EVIDENCE (Fig 21)

There is a photograph in Robin Gardiner's book on the conspiracy "*Titanic*

- The Ship That Never Sank", allegedly showing *Titanic* in 1911. It shows the ship on the fitting out wharf at Harland & Wolff with *Olympic's* open A deck arrangement, *Titanic's* 16 port hole layout for the C-deck focs'le and *Titanic's* shorter B Deck aft promenade. The author claims this to be photographic proof of one the two ships in the process of changing its identity as it shows some of the main features of both ships on the same ship. This is puzzling, especially as it was clearly an official Harland & Wolff photograph although it had no H&W ID number. These ID numbers were always written in ink onto the negative by hand in the bottom right corner and therefore showed up as white writing in the print. Consequently the photograph was sent digitally to the curator of the *Titanic* museum in Belfast and he very kindly replied that the date was incorrect; it was actually of *Olympic* and was taken on 10th April 1920 during her major refit following her service as a troop ship in WW1, being converted back to normal passenger configuration. His reply included a digital copy of the original and it was clear that Gardiner's published copy had been cropped to remove the ID number, H&W 778. Whether this was done as an honest mistake or as an attempt to support his conspiracy theory I will probably never know. All I can say is it did nothing to persuade me that the conspiracy was genuine!

THE ATTEMPT TO SAIL TO HALIFAX

The abortive attempt to sail the damaged ship to Halifax was probably a crucial factor in the sinking of the *Titanic*. If the conspiracy theory were true, one has to ask the question - how is it that J Bruce Ismay (who would most certainly have been a key figure in the conspiracy) did not say "Great, we have struck a real iceberg? We don't have to fake it any more!" As this clearly did not happen, that would indicate that the conspiracy was a fake too.

During my many years of presenting the *Titanic* story, I have occasionally had some remarkable feedback, usually from people who have a personal *Titanic* connection. One in particular relates to the conspiracy theory and undermines the story in a convincing way.

THE PREGNANT STEWARDESS

One evening I was giving a talk about *Titanic* in the community hall of a small town in Hampshire; when I finished and invited questions, an elderly gentleman in the front row (who I thought had slept through the entire occasion!) put up his hand and said "That conspiracy theory! Load of rubbish!" I asked what he meant by that, and out came the most wonderful story. He told us that, as a young woman, his grandmother had been a stewardess in the First Class section of *Olympic*. When she became unexpectedly pregnant she left the ship temporarily and went home to her family in Winchester to have the baby. On the way there, sitting in the train, she realised to her horror that she had left her sewing basket in her cabin locker on board the ship. That might not mean much today, but in those days for a woman in her line of work, her sewing basket represented a means of enhancing her wages considerably by doing occasional sewing jobs for her First Class passengers. But there was nothing to be done and she continued homeward. However, when she had had the baby, she returned to White Star's office in Southampton hoping she might have been rostered for *Titanic's* maiden voyage, something she had never experienced before. To her disappointment she was rostered back on *Olympic*, but when she reached her old cabin, there was her sewing basket still in her locker! Surely this was clear proof that the ships had not been switched.

CHAPTER 7
MYTHS, COMPLACENCY AND PLAIN BAD LUCK

THE FACTS: THE CREW

It is true that there was a situation at Plymouth where the SS *Lapland* had docked, which was bringing home the surviving crew members; the crew were then locked up in the dockside Third Class waiting room for three days and interviewed ('de-briefed' in modern parlance) one at a time by officials from the Board of Trade, the local Receiver of Wrecks and from White Star, and required or obliged to sign what we would call a 'non-disclosure agreement' but described at the time as 'the Official Secrets Act'. This was the second occasion the crew had been heartlessly delayed in re-joining their families. Although the conspiracy advocates eagerly grabbed this event as support for their story, it is much more likely that it was a part of White Star's efforts to cover up the Company's and the Board of Trade's alleged incompetence. Why else would they choose to use this small port (a normal stop for the east-bound SS *Lapland*) instead of taking the crew straight back to their families in Southampton, where most of them came from? (Fig 24).

It all seems most unkind, but it was actually vital for the company that the crew were prevented from any contact with the press, who were notorious then for fabricating and twisting the story to suit their editors' need to sell newspapers. The crew members were eventually released and taken by train to Southampton, where they received a rapturous welcome from their families and friends, though they also had to deal with the inevitable press circus. However, 34 of their fellow crew members were still in New York giving evidence at the Senate Inquiry.

Fig 24. *Titanic's* surviving crew held for 3 days at Plymouth Harbour station (UFT Museum)

THE FACTS: CREW PAY STOPPED

Another apparently shocking allegation made following the disaster was that White Star stopped the crew's pay at midnight on the day of the sinking. This is true. However, it was normal at that time; crew members signed the ship's articles on joining any ship and this was one of the conditions. The wording of the clause actually referred to pay stopping when the voyage ended, which would necessarily include the sinking of the ship! The clause still applies for many merchant shipping lines today.

THE MYTHS: POOR STEEL QUALITY

There have been numerous accusations that *Titanic* was built of poor quality steel and rivets; this is definitely an unfair and inaccurate allegation. It is understood that samples of *Titanic's* steel were taken from the wreck soon after its discovery in 1985, and that after examination were found to be examples of the highest quality of steel available at that time. The problem was that steel of that era was prone to becoming brittle at low temperatures such as in the North Atlantic, and that this may have contributed to the type and extent of the damage to *Titanic* when she struck the iceberg. Interestingly, steel technology regarding this brittleness did not change or improve until shortly after WW2, which tells us that Britain's entire naval force of warships throughout two world wars were probably built with same steel as *Titanic's*. The reality is that *Titanic* was built to standards of strength and quality way beyond what was demanded at the time. As *Titanic* historian and author Bruce Beveridge puts it "*Titanic* was designed and constructed with more than enough strength to sail the North Atlantic and withstand the heaviest gales known to man. *Titanic* was not designed to withstand freak accidents and she was not designed to sink!"

THE MYTHS: STEEL SPECIFICATION.

Some say that White Star (Ismay) changed the specification of the steel and rivets in order to save some weight (4,000 tons was mentioned) in order to extend the ships' endurance and range. It was alleged that the thickness of the hull plates was reduced by 1/8 inch and the diameter of the rivets by a similar amount. However, there is no real evidence for this happening, but the suggestion was a gift to the conspiracy theorists for obvious reasons.

THE MYTHS: HYMN "NEARER MY GOD TO THEE"

Many people think that the last music played by the ship's orchestra on the boat deck before the ship sank was the hymn *"Nearer my God to Thee".* There is no corroborative evidence for this, and it was most probably a romantic myth generated by the press. More reliable reports tell us the last music they played was ragtime dance music. Sadly, all the musicians died. Whatever music was being played had nothing to do with the disaster.

THE MYTHS: BLUE RIBAND

Some say that *Titanic* was trying to gain the Blue Riband as the fastest ship to cross the Atlantic. This is totally incorrect. The last time White Star held this accolade was with RMS *Teutonic* in 1891 at a speed of just over 20 knots, but in 1909 Cunard's brand new RMS *Mauretania* took the prize with a speed of almost 26 knots and kept it till 1929. White Star's three *Olympic* class ships had a design top speed of 23 knots, well short of the then-current Blue Riband holder's speed of 26 knots - a performance threshold that White Star no longer had an interest in attaining, as it would entail re-designing the ships with regard to hull profile, engine power and fuel capacity, all at huge additional cost.

THE MYTHS: THE MISSING KEY AND THE BINOCULARS

(Attorney General) *What do you think of binoculars for the look-out men?*

(Capt. Edward Cannons, Master Mariner) I *do not think they are any advantage at all. In the North Atlantic trade they would not be of much use because they are so easily blurred.*

(Attorney General) *It has been suggested here that binoculars should be used by the look-out men, particularly if they have had a report of ice. Will you tell my Lord your view about that?*

(Sir Ernest Shackleton) *My Lord, I do not believe in any look-out man having glasses at all. I only believe in the Officer using them, and then only when something has been reported in a certain quarter or certain place on the bow.*

London Inquiry Day 26

There were many fanciful myths and weird allegations about the disaster. One of them was the story of the key to the lookouts' binoculars cabinet on the bridge, accidentally taken from the ship by an officer who had been moved to another of the company's ships just before *Titanic's* maiden voyage.

David Blair was expecting to be appointed as Chief Officer (second in command) for *Titanic's* maiden voyage and was disappointed when William Murdoch (Fig 4) was appointed. But Murdoch was equally disappointed when Captain Smith decided at the last minute the position should be given to Henry Wilde (Fig 7) who had served with Captain Smith on *Olympic* for some time. The result was Blair was 'bumped off' the ship at Southampton and Murdoch was demoted to 1st Officer; Charles Lightoller(Fig 4) also had to step back one rank and take the position of 2nd Officer.

David Blair left the ship in such a hurry that he accidentally took an important key home with him. The key was allegedly from the cabinet in which the lookouts' binoculars were stored, although it first appeared in the Press as the key to the crow's nest telephone! (Figs 26a and 26b). It was not noticed as missing until the officer got home, by which time the *Titanic* had sailed and it was too late to return the key. This, it was claimed, meant the lookouts had no binoculars in the crow's nest which had prevented them from spotting the iceberg soon enough to prevent the collision. The Daily Telegraph published the story and announced they had found the cause of the *Titanic* disaster! It clearly shows what can be mistakenly achieved by land-lubber journalists with no real knowledge of maritime matters.

During my time in the Royal Navy I learned that lookouts were only rarely provided with binoculars; their task was to report anything significant seen with the naked eye to the bridge, from which point one of the officers would use binoculars to check the sighting. Spotting icebergs on a moonless night in an icy 22 knot wind from *Titanic's* crow's nest required the best available natural eyesight, which was perhaps why lookouts Fleet and Lee had been chosen. However, my understanding is that binoculars, which in those days had poor optics that absorbed about 15% of the available light anyway, would have been useless on a moonless night. This view was clearly supported in evidence given by Sir Ernest Shackleton.

In any event, we need to remember that it was only the key that was taken ashore; the binoculars were still in the cabinet, and if those locked-away binoculars had actually been needed, in all probability it would not have been difficult to find a crew member who knew how to pick such a simple lock!

THE RESULTS OF COMPLACENCY: WATERTIGHT BULKHEADS

Titanic's and *Olympic's* 15 watertight bulkheads were intended to protect the ship from extensive flooding in the event of serious hull damage. They would most probably do so satisfactorily in a head-on or beam-on collision with another vessel at sea. The longitudinal bulkheads in the 3 foot deep double bottom would certainly help to prevent the ship from listing after such a collision, a scenario that concerned ship owners and crew since it would have a serious effect on the ability to lower the lifeboats. This certainly proved to be the case for *Titanic*, as almost all her lifeboats were satisfactorily launched on both sides of the ship. There was a slight list to starboard of about 5 degrees after impact and then a list to port shortly before sinking, but this did not cause a problem with launching the boats.

The problem with the main watertight bulkheads was that they were not tall enough, extending on average to about 5 or 6 feet above the waterline. The designers had simply not envisaged the type and extent of damage that *Titanic* suffered as this kind of impact was virtually unknown and therefore was not factored in to the planning and the design.

Following the impact, as the forward compartments flooded, the ship's bow sank further into the water allowing the flooding to spill over into the next compartment. This caused further sinking of the bow and the next compartment flooded, and so on. This entire situation was massively worsened when Captain Smith ordered '*Slow Ahead*' 10 minutes after the impact. The result was tons of water being forced into the ruptured hull and significantly speeding up the 'ice tray' phenomenon (see Chapter 10). However, there is the view held by some, that even if the watertight bulkheads had been full height, the ship would still have sunk with 5 flooded compartments, albeit less rapidly.

THE RESULTS OF COMPLACENCY: THE COAL BUNKER FIRE

There was indeed a fire in coal bunker No. 10 which was in boiler room No. 6 against bulkhead No. 5. The fire is thought to have started just before the ship's sea trials, a day or so prior to the ship leaving Belfast for Southampton. The ship was officially handed over by H&W to White Star immediately after the successful sea trials, and the Company accepted her, handed over the cheque for £1.5M and continued with the plan for the maiden voyage, completely ignoring the fire, of which they must have been aware.

Most of the Belfast delivery crew left the ship and returned to Belfast, while a new crew, mostly based in Southampton, embarked for the maiden voyage. Also joining the crew were 12 additional stokers, specifically taken on to deal with the bunker fire.

But it was accepted as part of life on coal-fired steamers and the crew just got on with the job of putting the fire out, or more commonly, shovelling the burning coal into the nearest furnace, as in *Titanic's* case. In this instance the fire was extinguished by Saturday afternoon, the day before she hit the iceberg. We can see that the bunker fire was not allowed to affect the plans for the maiden voyage, and the passengers were almost certainly unaware of it. This may seem shocking to us today, bathed as we are in the ever-present 'Health and Safety' paradigm, but 100 years ago it was the normal way of dealing with a coal bunker fire.

On January 1st 2017, Channel 4 Television showed a programme "*Titanic – the New Evidence*" about how the author of a new book, the political editor of the Irish Daily Mail, Senan Molony, believed the bunker fire had been a key factor in the sinking of the *Titanic*. He claimed that the fire had severely weakened the hull to the extent that the relevant bulkhead collapsed during the sinking and that this hastened her demise, causing additional loss of life. He produced hitherto unseen photographic 'evidence' showing the ship departing from Belfast with a large black mark 75 feet long on her starboard side, below the forward well deck, claiming it to have been caused by the coal bunker fire. I disagreed with this viewpoint and made the following notes at the time:

"The story of the fire in coal bunker No. 10 is well known in 'Titaniac' circles; such fires were fairly common in those days especially with very tall narrow coal bunkers like *Titanic's* where the coal at the bottom was compressed by the many tons of coal above it, causing coal gas and methane to leak out and occasionally to combust spontaneously.

It is well-known that most of the stokers on the delivery crew for the trip to Southampton left the ship and returned to their homes to Belfast - as planned. A new crew, including a fresh team of stokers, was taken on at Southampton for the maiden voyage.

The dark mark on the starboard side of the ship is not conclusive evidence of the fire damage for the following reasons (Fig 25):

a. The mark appears to be approximately 75 feet long and extended from between 12 - 20 feet above the waterline. Although it seems to be in the same general area as the fire, it does not match the actual position, size or shape of the bunker fire. The coal bunker itself was only about 10ft wide though 50ft high, extended down to the lowest deck of the ship called the tank top, 30ft below the waterline, which is where any fire effects would have been - invisible from the surface! The fire was at the very bottom of the bunker by its very nature; the dark mark's aft-most limit was some 60 feet forward from the burning coal bunker and 40-50 feet above it. In other words, the mark was in the wrong place to have any significance at all. The bunker fire was far too small to have any serious weakening effect on the ship's massive structural strength.

b. It is well known that the port side of the ship was freshly painted at Harland & Wolff just prior to the maiden voyage, as this was the side that would be seen by the public and the passengers as they boarded at Southampton. The starboard side was left in 'dockyard scruff order' a) as it would not be seen by the passengers and b) the builders had run out of time prior to the maiden voyage. The dark mark can easily be explained as part of this situation, probably just a patch of fresh paint. If it had been caused by the bunker fire any resultant scorched paint would probably have been ash-grey, not shiny black."

In the programme, to imply that shovelling the burning coal into the furnaces caused the ship to "over-steam" and speed up too much does

Fig 25. Shows paint mark is over 60 feet from the coal bunker fire, and above the waterline.

not stand up to scrutiny. Apart from the absolute fact that the ship's engineers would be in full control of the ship's speed (subject to the Captain's orders), *Titanic* had 29 (mostly double ended) boilers. The fire was in just one bunker, No 10, which fed only 2 of the 4 boilers in boiler room No.6. At the time of the accident 5 of the 29 boilers were still unlit. In purely practical terms, the burning coal from No 10 bunker could only have been shovelled into the two nearest furnaces of one of the boilers in boiler room No.6. This would have had a minimal effect on the potential power output of *Titanic's* engines since this is controlled from the engine room, and not by the amount of coal being shovelled into the furnaces. Basically, the author, seems to have exaggerated the importance of the fire to support his contention that it was a significant factor in the sinking. By the time that bulkhead failed, if that is what happened, the ship was probably lost anyway, though the evidence strongly suggests that the watertight bulkheads failed due to overflow as a result of their inadequate height, not structural failure. While the coal bunker fire was an extremely unlikely contributor to the sinking, it demonstrates the arrogance and complacency of the owners in continuing with the maiden voyage.

BAD LUCK: SHORTAGE OF COAL

Since February 1912 there had been a coal miners' strike in Britain, which was extremely damaging for many industries, including shipping. *Titanic's* maiden voyage was under threat not to take place at all and White Star were very concerned. However there was no such strike in the US, and so RMS *Olympic* was used to bring back a load of coal on her previous return voyage. Sacks of coal were stacked into any empty cabins and then off-loaded at Southampton, but left a huge task for the cleaning staff on the ship! However, even when added to the White Star Company's coal storage depot at Southampton docks, this was not enough for *Titanic's* maiden voyage, so many tons were garnered from the five other White Star and IMM ships laid up in Southampton. Barge after barge came alongside *Titanic* and manually loaded hundreds of tons of coal into *Titanic's* bunkers, a task universally hated by officers and crew alike. Interestingly, this process included topping up No 10 coal bunker, effectively stoking

Fig 26a. Crow's nest telephone key (Daily Telegraph)

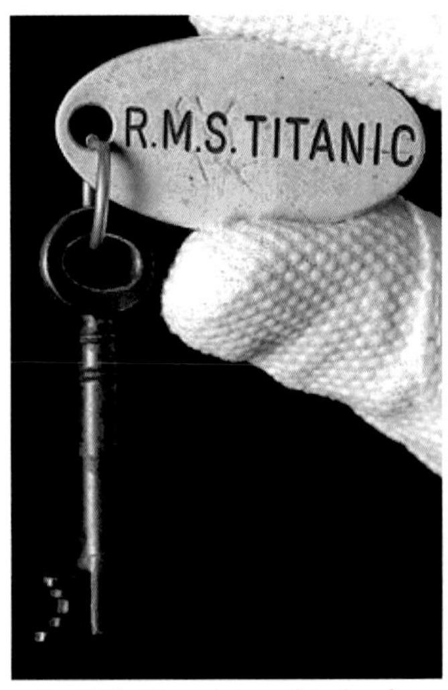

Fig 26b. Key claimed to be for crow's nest binoculars (Daily Telegraph)

the bunker fire that had been burning there for almost a week. With 2 days of coal in reserve, *Titanic* was not short of coal, but the country was. However, the coal shortage, while interesting, had absolutely no bearing on the sinking.

Fig 27. SS *Carpathia* in New York following the rescue (Robin Gardiner)

Fig 28. Engelhardt collapsible lifeboat D coming alongside SS *Carpathia* (Frances Wilson)

Fig 29. Lifeboat No 6 approaching SS *Carpathia* with QM Hichens on the helm (Walter Lord)

Fig 30. SS *Mackay-Bennett's* crew recovering upturned collapsible lifeboat B (W Lord)

Fig 31. With their double bottom and 16 watertight compartments, the *Olympic* Class ships were heralded as being their own lifeboat. (Walter Lord)

CHAPTER 8
THE LIFEBOATS

It is not intended to give the reader a detailed 'chapter and verse' on the order of launching of the lifeboats or how many and who each boat contained, as that information is readily available elsewhere. But the fact that only 3 of the boats were filled close to capacity (60+) and most of the others were less than half-filled needs some explanation.

As you will read later, Captain Smith was aware of the number of lifeboats available to him, and he was utterly shocked and horrified at the situation he was faced with. The designers and owners had simply not envisaged this kind of calamity. After all, the ship was 'unsinkable' with her double-bottomed hull and 15 watertight bulkheads. Yet Smith had lifeboat spaces for only 1178 of the 2200 people in his care. How in heavens' name could this happen?

After the collision, Smith briefed his officers to minimize the chance of causing alarm to the passengers by saying, "help is on the way (which was true) and launching the lifeboats is just a precaution (which was not true)". His actual plan was to get as many lifeboats on the water as soon as possible, though partly filled to save time. He was acutely aware that in the limited time the ship had left it would be impossible to launch all the boats with a full passenger load. He wanted all the boats on the water so that they could be ready to pick up survivors after the ship had gone. A situation whereby lifeboats could be lost in the sinking was not to be contemplated.

There was an interesting dimension to this approach as most of the officers and crew were unfamiliar with the launching procedure due to their lack of training, and they seemed to be convinced the boats and tackle would not take the weight of a full passenger load whilst hanging from the davits. (The design of the boats and the Welin system was actually more than up to the task, it was later revealed). 5th Officer Lowe told the inquiry in New York that he felt that the maximum number of passengers that could be safely lowered in a lifeboat was 50. Even if Smith had ordered full boats to be launched, he may not have had time to achieve the desired result anyway.

After some of the boats were launched, Smith himself used a loud hailer to try to bring some of them alongside to take off more passengers through the open loading door in the ship's side, which he could see was now almost at water level and would have to be closed very soon. No one in the boats seemed to hear him nor understand what he was saying.

As mentioned, Smith's plan was to have the partly-loaded boats ready to pick up survivors in the water, but even this part of his planning was scuppered; he may have given the instruction for this to happen, but it failed to reach those in the boats, where there was a mixed reaction to their predicament. Some of crew handling the boats refused to go back to the wreck site and pick up people in the water, fearing their boat might capsize in the process; Quartermaster Hichens (Fig 29) was notable among these and had a serious confrontation with the famous Molly Brown who threatened to throw him overboard, while in other boats, the reverse happened with the passengers preventing the crew from returning.

There was one exception to this; 5th Officer Lowe, without any resistance from his crew or his passengers, is the only known person to take his lifeboat, No 16, back to look for survivors still alive in the water; he found only five.

Though not actually lifeboats, No's 1 and 2 (40-place 'emergency' boats) nevertheless were included in the overall count of lifeboats on *Olympic* and *Titanic*. No.1 lifeboat contained only 12 people. They comprised Mr Duff-Gordon, owner of a well-known gin distillery, his wife and her secretary, and their daughter. Seven crewmen had been ordered into the boat as crew. There are different versions of the story, and it is unclear whether Duff-Gordon paid the crewmen £20 to find him a lifeboat or that he paid them £5 each after they had been picked up by *Carpathia*. One could take the view that either he had effectively 'bought' a lifeboat for himself and his family, or that he was sympathetic to the crews' situation of losing their pay after the sinking and wished to make a generous gesture. The latter view seems the more likely.

In the event, it seems that very few survived being in the water, dying from hypothermia shortly after being rescued. 2nd Officer Lightoller did survive, but sadly, 20 or so of those on the list of the dead were actually in the lifeboats.

The following day, a number of ships arrived at the scene to help pickup any bodies and remaining boats (Fig 30). The bodies of steerage and Second Class passengers were usually left; only First Class passengers were lifted out for future burial, the distinction being made by appearances only.

There has been a great deal of discussion around the survival rate of the various social classes on board; clearly one had the highest chance of survival if one was a First Class passenger at 63%. The lowest survival rate shows the crew at 23% ; this included the loss of the entire engine room watch of 35 men. Over the entire disaster, 36% of the survivors were men, the rest being the women and children. Clearly, the British class system was alive and well in 1912, although the 'Birkenhead Drill' of 'women and children first' also still applied.

CHAPTER 9
THE COLLISION

(Senator Duncan to Charles Lightoller): *"I will get you to state, not only from your actual knowledge of the immediate effect, but also from your experience as a navigator and seaman, what the effect of that collision was on the ship, beginning with the first effect, the immediate effect; how it listed the ship, if it did; what effect it had then, and what in your opinion was the effect on the ship that resulted from that collision." Mr Charles Lightoller: "The result was the ship sank."*

In spite the Senator's pompous and verbose style of questioning, for which he was well-known, Lightoller deflated him with the simplest of replies!

The lookouts Fleet and Lee had been on watch in the crow's nest for over an hour and a half. With the 25 mph icy wind in their faces for that length of time they must have felt frozen half to death. Yet they saw the iceberg in spite of there being no actual wind to produce wavelets at the iceberg's base. It was also what sailors called a 'blue berg', one with a darkened bottom which had rolled over exposing its original underside, embedded with soil, rocks and plants from its thousands of years scraping its way down the glacial valley which formed it.

There have been various estimates of the range at which the iceberg was first seen by the lookouts, varying from 4 minutes to 90 seconds. If we take the closest possible scenario of 90 seconds, then even so, there should have been sufficient time for *Titanic* to turn away and avoid the iceberg (Fig 32). We know from her trials that *Titanic's* smallest turning circle had a diameter of 1.9 nautical miles (2.2 statute miles at 20 knots). If full port helm was put over immediately there would have been a 30 second delay before the ship responded, due to the complicated operating mechanism of cables and chains between the ship's wheel and the push-pull steam steering engines that moved the tiller. This then left 40 seconds for the ship to actually turn, in which case it has been estimated she should have cleared the iceberg by 100 -200 yards (Fig 32). Why did this not happen? How is it that *Titanic* hit the berg with that amount of time available for the rudder and engine responses and for the ship to turn? Even more curious, how did this happen if the range from the first sighting was actually greater than our assumed 'worse case scenario', as many people claim? Was the ship's response affected by Murdoch's engine room order "Stop engines" followed by "Full astern both"?

HARD A'STARBOARD!

1st Officer William Murdoch was Officer of the Watch when the call came through from the crow's nest "Iceberg dead ahead!" He immediately ordered the quartermaster "Hard a'starboard!". That may sound strange to us since we know that the ship needed to turn to port (left) to avoid the iceberg, so why did Murdoch order a turn to starboard (right)?

The order was normal and correct in those days for a left hand (port) turn. The reason was that in 1912 shipping was in a mixed state of sailing and steam vessels. In sailing ships, helm orders were given as 'tiller' orders; in other words, if you wished to turn your sailing boat or ship to port, you put the tiller over to the starboard side. When wheel steering was introduced, they continued to use tiller orders to avoid confusion. It was the steering convention that nearly all sailors had been trained on at that time. Hence an urgent turn to port was called as "hard a'starboard" so the tiller was turned to starboard, although the wheel was actually turned to port. This protocol continued in use on steam ships long after commercial sailing vessels had disappeared, but because it caused confusion, as well as a few accidents, it was abandoned by the Merchant Marine Service in 1931 and by the Royal Navy a few years later.

Gradually *Titanic* responded, but by then she was just too close to the iceberg and was thought to have run over an underwater shelf of ice, rather like a car going over a speed bump. The impact was relatively gentle and many people were unaware anything had happened. But the result was thought to be an intermittent gash extending over 300 feet in the ship's double bottom, opening up four, possibly five, watertight compartments from the foc'sle to underneath the bridge (Fig 33). However, we must remember that the ice shelf and the 300-foot gash theories are both just that – un-provable theories; the ship's damaged bottom is buried deep in the Atlantic mud, and the iceberg has long since melted away! But it is the most plausible explanation. The question still arises, 'why did she hit the iceberg?' According to the worst-case scenario, following the call from the crow's nest, 1st Officer Murdoch had 90 seconds to turn the ship away from the iceberg – a minute and a half. Other estimates of the distance to the iceberg suggest up to 4 minutes warning. What went wrong? There were even reports of 'no response' to earlier calls from the lookouts over the previous 25 minutes, but this is not confirmed by Fleet's and Lee's evidence at the London Inquiry:

(The Attorney General): *Before half-past eleven on that watch - that is, seven bells - had you reported anything at all, do you remember?*

(Lookout Reginald Lee): *There was nothing to be reported.*

(Attorney General): *Then what was the first thing you did report?*

(Reginald Lee): *The first thing that was reported was after seven bells struck; it was some minutes, it might have been nine or ten minutes afterwards. Three bells were struck by Fleet, warning "Right ahead," and immediately he rung the telephone up to the bridge, "Iceberg right ahead." The reply came back from the bridge, "Thank you."*

(The Commissioner): *This would be about 11.40?*

(Reginald Lee): *Yes* London Inquiry Day 4

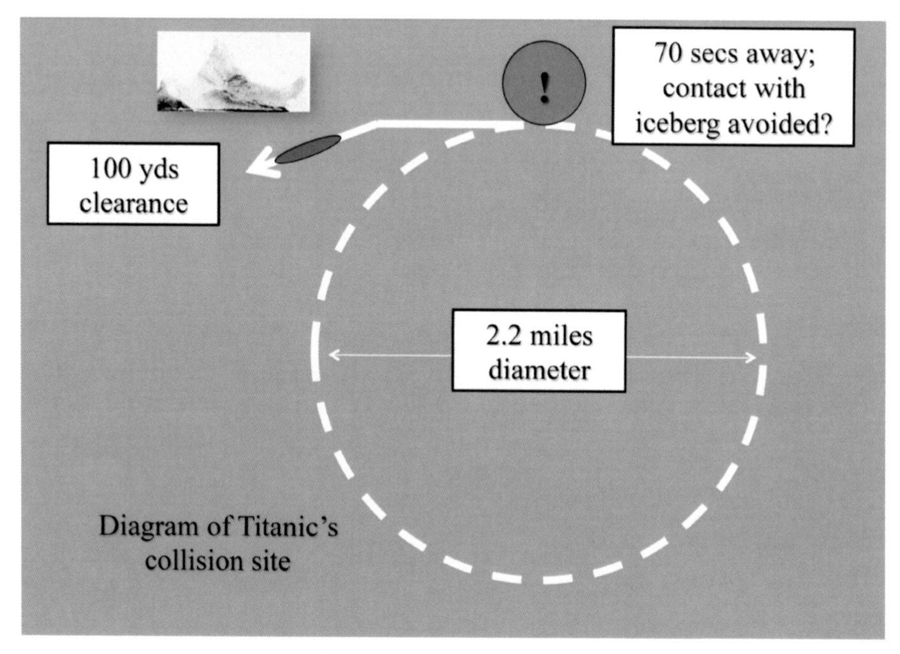

Fig 32. Diagram showing how *Titanic's* turning circle and how she would have missed the iceberg, even with only 90 seconds warning (worst case scenario quoted). (Author)

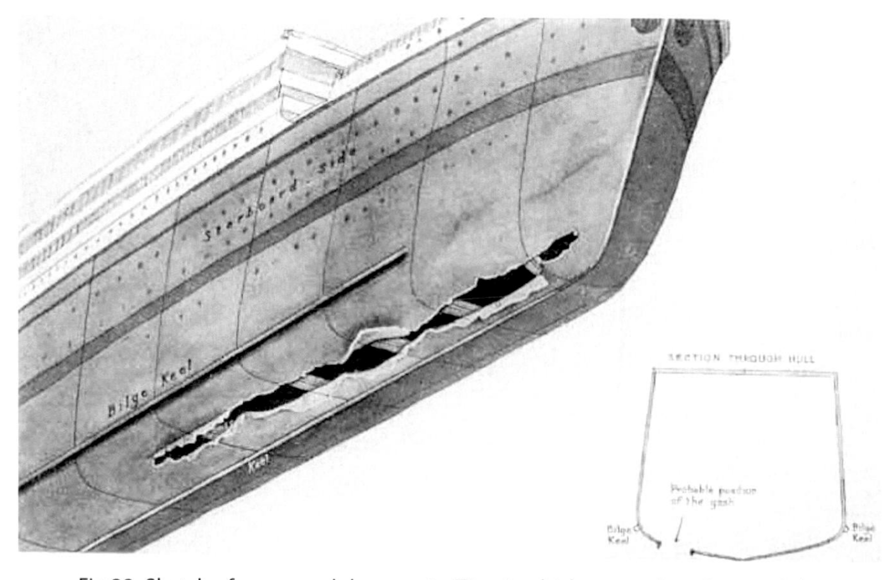

Fig 33. Sketch of presumed damage to *Titanic* which opened up 5 watertight compartments (Frances Wilson)

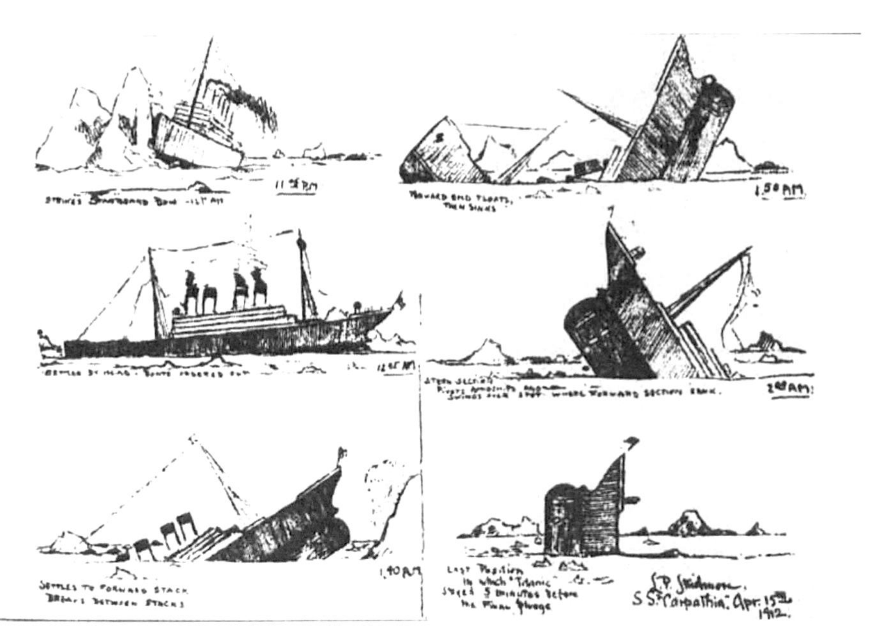

Fig 34. 16 year-old Jack Thayer's description of the sinking shows her 'sagging' not 'hogging' as generally thought, re-drawn by LD Skidmore on the SS *Carpathia*. (Robert Ballard)

Titanic hit the iceberg at 23:41 ship's time; all watertight doors were closed from the bridge by Murdoch and the ship was stopped. Captain Smith came out of the chart room, which was abaft the wheelhouse, asking what has happened. "We hit an iceberg, sir" replied Murdoch. "I tried to port around it but we were too close". "Have you closed the watertight doors?" asked Smith. "Watertight doors all closed, sir".

Minutes later other people appeared on the bridge; Lightoller was still in his pyjamas and slippers, and Smith asked Chief Engineer Bell, who had come up from his cabin, for a damage report. He set off to assess the damage with Thomas Andrews. J Bruce Ismay came in from his stateroom just behind the bridge. Smith told him what had happened and they went into the chart room to discuss the situation.

The following part of the story was never told at the inquiries. As a result it was not mentioned in either of the reports, yet it was a crucial part of the disaster in terms of survival and questionable seamanship. Even more extraordinary, it fitted in nicely with what many regarded as the inquiries' pre-determined decision to blame Captain Smith and yet it was not used as such. It was probably the only serious error of judgment by Captain Smith during the whole sorry affair. This is what happened:

J Bruce Ismay suggested that since they were only 400 miles away from the nearest major port, Halifax, Nova Scotia, it might be a good idea to set a course in that direction. "Even if we proceed slowly, we could be there by tomorrow afternoon" he declared. Smith was most probably very unhappy about this, but since Ismay was in effect *Titanic's* owner and Smith was the employee, he went along with the plan.

At 11:50 the engines were re-started and this was heard by many passengers. Smith rang down to the engine room 'Slow ahead both' and the ship moved off on a north-westerly course. Fifteen minutes later it was obvious the ship was much further down by the head; the split in the hull having effectively scooped up hundreds of tons of water by the ships' forward movement and she had now passed the 'tipping point'. Then the damage reports came in to the bridge and it was clear the ship was doomed, although Bell and Andrews estimated she could float for an hour and a half (it was actually two hours and forty minutes). Smith must have really regretted going along with Ismay's plan. It would seem that this was the only significant error of judgment he made for it is now clear that if *Titanic* had stayed where she was, rescue may well have arrived in time and maybe no one would have died. Some may doubt the accuracy of this part of the story, but it was reported in the Montreal 'Evening Sun' that:

" Montreal, April 15 - at 8.30 o'clock an unofficial despatch (sic) reached Montreal from Halifax, stating that the Titanic was still afloat and was making her way slowly towards Halifax."

Later that day the Dow Jones News Service in New York made the following announcement:

"Arrangements have been made with New Haven Railroad Company to send a special train to Halifax, Nova Scotia to meet passengers from the 'Titanic'. It will consist of 11 sleepers. 2 diners and coaches for 710 people"

From the ship, Senior Marconi Operator Jack Phillips sent a telegram to his parents in Godalming, Surrey which said: *"Making slowly for Halifax. Practically unsinkable. Don't worry - Jack".* Sadly, this message arrived at Mr and Mrs Phillips home a few hours after they had learned that Jack was not on the list of survivors. He had died in a lifeboat from hypothermia.

The ship was now clearly sinking, though at a slower rate than Bell and Andrews had anticipated earlier. Smith gave the order to uncover the lifeboats and prepare the passengers to board them, but also to tell them help was on the way and launching the boats was simply a precautionary action, so as not to alarm them.

However, he was more than conscious of the fact there were only enough lifeboats for about half the souls on board and he would have to think very carefully how to manage that. He had been advised by Bell and Andrews that the ship would probably stay afloat for only an hour and a half, and he knew that that was insufficient time to load and launch all the boats; it simply could not be done, so he came up with a plan to launch the boats but only partly-filled to save time. The boats would then all be on the water ready to pick up survivors after the ship had gone. He also realised that the majority of his passengers and crew were about to die, and there could be no place in a lifeboat for him; he would almost certainly go down with his ship. The partly-filled lifeboats became the subject of much debate; was this due to the lack of crew training (a very reasonable supposition in the circumstances), or was it due to selfishness and cowardice on the part of the boats' occupants, passengers or crew? There were several reports of such attitudes when the boats were on the water; some passengers wanted to go back to pick up survivors, just as Smith had planned, but often the crew refused for fear of swamping or capsizing the boat. The same also occurred the other way round, with passengers, some of whom were very rich and powerful, preventing the more sympathetic crew from returning to the site of the sinking. However, boat No 16 under the command of 5th Officer Lowe, who had already 'rafted up' a small group of lifeboats and evened out their occupancy, did go back, but he found only 5 survivors alive in the water, one of whom died shortly afterwards.

No one knows for certain what happened to Captain Smith, but many think that he was probably killed when No 1 funnel collapsed onto the bridge, shortly before she sank. The same fate may well have befallen Chief Officer Wilde and 1st Officer Murdoch, since the bridge is most probably where they would have been standing at the time.

It has been said by some commentators, usually those with some understanding of the principles of naval architecture, that if *Titanic* had run head-on into the iceberg instead of trying to swerve around it, the ship would most probably have survived. I am reliably informed that that may well have been the case, although all agree that there would have been a heavy death/injury price to pay as the forward-most compartments of the forecastle crumpled with many crew and Third Class passengers inside. How extensive this would be is a matter for an experienced naval architect to calculate, and would be conditional on the unknown factor of the ship's actual speed at the moment she would have struck.

Following this line of thought, it was recorded during her sea trials that *Titanic* could come to a dead stop under a "Full astern both engines" order in 850 feet, which took 3 minutes and 15 seconds.

One wonders why Murdoch did not attempt this with the quoted worst-case scenario of 912 yards (2,736 feet) away when the iceberg was first sighted. But we have to factor in the response times of the lookouts, Murdoch on the bridge and the engineers on the controls in the engine room, each of whom could easily, and understandably, lose several precious seconds in their reactions. We also have to bear in mind that the engines were running initially at 75 revolutions and would have to be slowed down, stopped and then re-started in reverse. It seems highly likely, since Murdoch was a very experienced officer, that he felt there was simply was not enough time or distance available to complete such a manoeuvre safely, and he chose the naturally instinctive option of trying to avoid a collision completely. This also suggests that the worst-case scenario of around 90 seconds warning might have been close to being the correct one.

WAS TITANIC A WEAK SHIP?

Since the sinking over 100 years ago there have been literally dozens of comments and accusations about *Titanic's* strength and her suitability for trans-Atlantic travel. The matter was discussed at length at both the Inquiries. However, it is interesting to see that the source for such information appears to have come, in the main, from two non-seafaring groups; the members of the Inquiry Boards and the Press.

The most common accusation against White Star and Harland & Wolff was that *Olympic's* and *Titanic's* hulls were weak, allegedly having been built from sub-standard or low specification steel. Included in this was the accusation that the 2 expansion joints in the superstructure formed weak points in the hull and actually caused the hull to break in two as she sank. The origin for these points came from a mischievous report that *Titanic* was reported, and allegedly noted by Thomas Andrews, to be 'panting' during her sea trials in Belfast Lough. In reality, panting would only be detectable in a seriously rough sea and this did not happen during her trials. No such note exists in the records (as it most certainly would have been if true). Added to which, metallurgical tests on steel samples from the wreck show it was the correct steel specification and of the highest quality of steel available at that time.

When *Olympic's* double bottom was extended up the sides of the ship during her 1912 refit, suspicions were raised as to the integrity of *Titanic's* hull. Other changes in 1912 included increasing the height of 5 of her watertight bulkheads up to the weather decks, and a dividing bulkhead in the electric engine room. The upward extension of the double bottom included only the hull sections containing the machinery spaces and boilers and went several feet above the waterline. Accusers believed it was a sign of inherent hull weakness being rectified, but the truth was White Star wanted to improve the ship's watertight integrity, with the bonus of reducing the possibility of her hull being penetrated, a move thoroughly vindicated when she was struck by a dud torpedo in 1918. Not generally known at the time, but White Star and H&W were aware that *Olympic's* boilers and furnaces would be converting to oil-burning in the near future, and the new double skin was constructed to allow for the fitting of fuel oil storage tanks. The inner skin's construction and attachment to the outer hull was such that it was not possible, nor was it designed, to stiffen or strengthen the ship.

A feature of *Titanic* not included in *Olympic's* 1912 changes was the screening-in of the forward half of the A-Deck promenade, and there seems to be no explanation for this. What is known is that this also was not fitted to stiffen or strengthen *Titanic* as many have alleged; it was far too lightly built for that. It was simply to provide extra weather protection for the First Class passengers, as declared by the Company at the time.

Edward Wilding, Thomas Andrews' successor, made two crucial statements some time later. Firstly, that the alleged weakness of the hull caused by the two expansion joints was made by those who had no understanding of naval architecture. The expansion joints were only in the 'relatively weaker' super-structure to accommodate any minor flexing of the main hull. If that superstructure were to be removed from ship, the main hull would be just as strong and rigid. Secondly, he stated that "We have had less repairs to the *Olympic* than to any large ship we have ever built, due to external causes, of course".

All these facts leave this author in no doubt that the *Olympic* Class ships were built up to and beyond all the strength requirements placed upon the designers and builders. They were, as historian Bruce Beveridge states, "designed to sail the Atlantic, but not to survive a collision with an iceberg". No ship ever was, in just the same way that no aircraft could ever be designed to survive a mid-air collision.

CHAPTER 10
HOW DID TITANIC SINK AND BREAK UP?

The designers of the *Olympic* class ships had tried very hard to anticipate all the possible accident or collision scenarios that these huge ships might encounter. They looked at head-on collision and side-impact, but they were not familiar with the principle of running over 'speed bumps' that we see today on our roads, but that is more or less what happened to *Titanic*, so far as we can tell. It is impossible to say for certain as the damaged area is buried deep into the Atlantic's sea bed. However, since there is no evidence of impact damage to *Titanic's* visible hull plates on the starboard side of the wreck, the torn-open ship's bottom seems to be the most likely damage. It is also true to say that if *Titanic* had hit the iceberg with the side of the ship, there would have been a noticeable sideways 'bump' which everyone on board would have felt, but this was not the case. In spite of the current arguments among the experts about this, it makes no difference to the outcome. She sank.

The designers did a lot of work trying to prevent the ships from adopting a serious list in the event of flooding by placing longitudinal bulkheads within the double bottom and in the lower decks, and this worked well on *Titanic*, which took on a 5 degree list to starboard that apparently did not interfere too much with launching the lifeboats. As she sunk deeper, she rolled into a slight list to port before the final plunge.

Not unreasonably, the possibility of an ice shelf, hidden 30 feet below the surface, was not anticipated by the Harland & Wolff design team. The impact lasted for about 10 seconds during which time the ice had apparently ripped open a 300 foot gash in the ship's bottom from the bow to under the bridge, piercing the double skin and opening up 5 watertight compartments (Fig 33). (Whilst the impact with the ice shelf cannot be proved, it is the most plausible explanation and may be accepted as true.) The steel used at that time tended to become brittle at such low temperatures and this possibly contributed to the extent of the damage. Designer Thomas Andrews stressed that she could probably stay afloat for hours if only four compartments had been ruptured. But the fifth flooded compartment gave them only 1½ to 2 hours, he thought, even with the pumps going flat out, and no real chance of saving her. Readers may recall that the 35 engineer officers stayed at their posts in the engine room to keep the electric generators running for the pumps and the deck lighting which was so essential to launching the lifeboats safely, an almost impossible task otherwise in total darkness. All those brave engineers, including Chief Engineer Bell, knew they would go down with the ship, but remained so that as many passengers as possible could be saved. There is a memorial to these 35 brave men in the centre of Southampton (see inside back cover).

As the ship sank lower and lower by the bow, water flowed over each bulkhead and flooded the next compartment, worsening the situation. The bulkheads were only a few feet higher than the waterline. This was another possible issue not foreseen by the designers, although *Titanic* was supposed to be 'her own lifeboat' and 'virtually unsinkable'!

Although unconnected with the actual collision, there are two versions of how she broke up on the surface while sinking; the high angle sinking and the low angle sinking. In the first scenario, as the bow began to sink under the sea, the hull could not take the strain and started to flex. The supporting wires of funnel No 1 snapped and the funnel collapsed onto the bridge, probably killing all inside, most likely including Captain Smith. The ship continued to flex so that the superstructure started to break up on the surface through the weakest part of the hull, aft of funnel No3, by 'hogging', and then sank in two pieces. This would mean that the upper part of the ship broke under tension and the keel broke under compression.

In the low angle version, after the collapse of the funnel, as water flooded further and deeper into the length of the hull, again the keel could not take the strain as the structure of the frames and scantlings were designed to take the ship's weight afloat, not in a reversal situation with the ship flooded internally. She broke her back, but with the centre section of the keel flexing downwards.

It has to be said that this second low angle version was never considered as a possibility until the discovery in 2003 of two 90 foot-wide sections of the ship's double bottom, lying some 500 metres from the main wreck (Fig 40). The huge fragments were discovered by divers Ritchie Kohler and John Chatterton in a chartered Mir submarine guided by lawyer David Concannon, a wealthy *Titanic* 'tourist' who had seen the fragments on a previous dive in 2000.

When the information surfaced about this third piece of the ship, it showed convincingly that the ship actually broke apart by 'sagging'. This was a huge shock for *Titanic* followers as it contradicted the popular view described by many surviving passengers, but the recently discovered pieces of her bottom proves that to be wrong; when the broken-off edges of the fragment were examined it was clear that the steel had been broken under tension, snapping-off cleanly, as steel always does in a tension fracture (Fig 40). However, when the broken edges of the upper levels of the superstructure are examined one can see the explosive effect of a compression steel fracture, all confirming the way the hull broke up during the sinking (Fig 39).

Which is the correct explanation of how *Titanic* broke up? The high angle 'hogging' version is without doubt the more popular, showing the power of the media and the imagination, but the science tells us that the low angle 'sagging' break up is possibly more accurate, especially since a series of sketches came to light drawn by a passenger, L D Skidmore, following a precise description of the sinking by 16 year-old student Jack Thayer on the SS *Carpathia*, shortly after being rescued from a lifeboat. There are no such images, contemporaneous or otherwise, of the high angle version (Fig 34).

It is interesting to note that *Titanic's* break-up on the surface is not mentioned by 2nd Officer Charles Lightoller, nor by several other survivors, at either of the inquiries. The question remains, did she break up on the surface as so many have said, or did she break up after she sank? The official and most acceptable opinion is that she broke up as, and because, she sank; she did not sink because she broke up.

CHAPTER 11
THE INQUIRIES

THE US SENATE INQUIRY:

IN THE SENATE OF THE UNITED STATES, April 17th 1912

Resolved, That the Committee on Commerce, or a subcommittee thereof, is hereby authorized and directed to investigate the causes leading to the wreck of the White Star liner *Titanic*, with its attendant loss of life so shocking to the civilized world.

QUOTATION FROM THE US SENATE INQUIRY:

(Senator Smith to Charles Lightoller): *"At what time did you leave the ship?"*

(Charles Lightoller): *"I did not leave the ship. The ship left me".*

Many commentators have viewed the inquiries with suspicion, saying the outcome was pre-determined, even before the inquiries had heard any evidence. One remarkable fact was that although *Titanic* was a British vessel, built and registered in Britain with an almost entirely British crew and a predominately British passenger list, the US government failed to notify the British Embassy in Washington that a US Senate inquiry into the disaster was to take place (Fig 35). The British ambassador, Sir James Bryce, commented to the press *"It would have been more courteous if some communication had been addressed to this Embassy".* The explanation for this desperately undiplomatic gaffe by the Americans was probably due to there being a very small number of rich and influential American passengers on board.

SHIP'S LOG

The maritime equivalent of modern aviation's 'black box' is the ship's log. It is a legally required detailed document of all the ship's major navigational movements and activities, and would be kept on the bridge or in the chartroom, at the heart of the ship's operations. Daily occurrences, such as the ship's position, speed, a change of course, sighting a vessel, or a change in the weather or sea state, would be quickly noted in a rough or 'scrap' log, and this would be transferred to the official log at the end of the watch or the day. Entries in the official log cannot be edited or erased; any necessary changes to the text in the log have to be signed for by the entrant, and the original text must be left in place and legible. Responsibility for maintaining the official log normally lies with the Chief Officer, or in his absence, the Officer of the Watch, though this varies from ship to ship. There are strict rules regarding the logs in the event of imminent disaster; in wartime, they would be destroyed to prevent the capture by the enemy of sensitive information. In peacetime, in the event of an impending disaster, the ship's logs would be ready to be placed in the first lifeboat by the responsible officer. As already mentioned, on a large vessel there would probably be two other logs subject to the same conditions, the Engine Room log and the Signals log, and attempts would normally be made to dispose of or salve these in the same way.

My understanding is that the care and management of the ship's logs would be covered by the Ship's Standing Orders, and I find it incomprehensible that the first question at each inquiry was not *"Do you have the ship's logs, and if not, where are they"?* There is no mention of the *Titanic's* logs in the transcript of either inquiry, so it is clear that this crucial question was never actually asked.

If the logs had been produced at the inquiries, so many crucial questions would have been immediately answered, and responsibility and blame could have been appropriately and honestly apportioned. I find it fascinating that not only are the logs not really mentioned at the inquiries, they are virtually absent from the text of any of the books I have read so far, with one ironic exception; Robin Gardiner discusses briefly how the logs may possibly have been placed into the collapsible lifeboat B and were subsequently lost when it capsized. This is pure conjecture of course as there is no supporting evidence, but it could possibly explain the mystery.

THE CREW

During the US Senate inquiry, *Titanic's* surviving officers and crew members were virtually imprisoned in a separate New York hotel, forbidden to leave the US, in spite of their desperation to return to their distraught families at home in England. Most of the passengers were permitted to continue to their various destinations, though some significant individuals, such as J Bruce Ismay and Mrs Molly Brown were also detained and, along with the crew, subpoenaed to attend the US inquiry.

THE CHAIRMAN

The chairman of the US Senate sub-committee in New York, Republican Senator William Alden Smith, was a curious choice since he had no sea-going maritime experience or expertise. He ran the US inquiry as his own show and seldom deferred to the six other senators on the Board, inducing some of them to attend only very occasionally.

Senator Smith was criticised extensively by the press and lampooned by cartoonists. Examples of his ineptitude as chairman of this particular inquiry include asking 5th Office Lowe *"Of what is an iceberg composed?"*. He said to 2nd Officer Lightoller *"This morning you said she (Titanic) went down by the head. Now you are saying she went down by the bow. Please make up your mind; which is it?"* He later asked Lightoller *"could they (the passengers) not, as a last resort, have taken refuge in a watertight compartment?".*
He was rapidly dubbed 'Watertight Smith' by the press.

While giving evidence in New York, J Bruce Ismay stated that he did not see *Titanic* sink and so could not say whether or not she broke up on the surface. Ismay explained he was *"rowing away from the ship and did not see her go down."* Apart from the improbability of this evidence, we all know that if he had been rowing away he would actually have been facing the ship as he rowed, but Senator Smith never picked up on the inconsistency, such was his ignorance of ships and the sea. However, Ismay explained later that since there was insufficient space available in the lifeboat to sit normally, he was assisting another passenger by pushing on the oar, and so having his back to the sinking ship.

US SENATE REPORT

Surprisingly, Senator Smith's report to the Senate, the outcome of the Sub-Committee's 18-day inquiry, contained all the items it should have contained, culminating in demands for massive changes and new ideas within maritime law. The list of new regulations included a compulsory 24-hour radio watch for all ships equipped with radio, speeding through ice fields was forbidden, a legal requirement for sufficient lifeboats for all on board any vessel, and a maritime patrol by the US Coastguard was set up to warn shipping of icebergs that continues to this day.

Captain Smith and the British Board of Trade both came in for heavy criticism at the New York inquiry, due to the inadequate number of lifeboats and the conclusion Captain Smith was navigating his ship at too high a speed for the conditions without posting extra lookouts. We need to remember, however, that it was the Board of Trade that had signed off *Titanic* as fit for her voyage in all respects, in spite of the inadequate number of lifeboats, and they therefore had a considerable vested interest as to how the London inquiry might be 'managed'.

THE LONDON INQUIRY

(The Attorney-General.) *You said it was not the "Titanic". Did you give him (your Marconi operator) any directions? Did you tell him to let the "Titanic" know?*

(Captain Lord of SS *Californian*). *I said, "Let the "Titanic" know that we are stopped, surrounded by ice."*

(The Attorney-General.) *Do you remember at what time that message was sent?*
(Captain Lord) *About 11 o'clock.*

(London Inquiry Day 7)

It is interesting to see that the London inquiry (Fig 36), chaired by the British Commissioner for Wrecks, Sir John Charles Bigham, Lord Mersey, was formed under the aegis of the British Board of Trade, the government organization that had inspected with full oversight the *Titanic* build programme over 2000 times, as well as having signed the ship off at Southampton as "in all respects fit for the intended voyage, and that the requirements under the merchant Shipping Acts have been complied with." No wonder the Board's possible motives for a favourable outcome were regarded as questionable.

As at the US Inquiry, no one asked any of the witnesses at the London inquiry as to where the *Titanic's* logs might be. If the logs had been saved and produced at the inquiries, many days of interrogation could have been avoided. Witnesses would not have had to rely on their memory for the most basic facts regarding the ship's position, speed, course, etc. in the hours leading up to the accident. Any navigational issues would have been apparent and evidential contradictions avoided or explained. I find this lack of questioning one of the most significant mysteries of the entire story.

One of the more important issues examined was the fact that the SS *Californian* did not go to *Titanic's* rescue. She was supposedly stuck in an ice field several nautical miles to the north, the actual distance having been the subject of much discussion over the years. Her officers saw a ship away to the south "sending up white flares about 4 to 7 nautical miles away". This was reported to Captain Lord who at the time was asleep in his cabin. Lord asked if they were distress rockets and was told they were not certain but thought it was possible; a series of 7 rockets had been seen and logged. The officers tried to contact the ship by Morse lamp but received no reply. No further action was ordered by the Captain as the ship appeared to sail away and disappear.

There is evidence that *Titanic* tried to contact "the vessel seen to the north" by Morse lamp at more or less the same time. They too received no response. A possible explanation lies in the knowledge that at that time there was an unusual meteorological condition in that area known as a 'temperature inversion' which probably was the cause of the slight haze at sea level. It could also have caused ships' lights and signal lamps to appear to flicker, rendering any attempt at Morse code by lamp totally unreadable.

(Examiner Mr. A T Rowlatt.) *Did you get any reply?*

(Third Officer Groves of the SS *Californian). Not at first, no reply whatsoever.*

(Examiner Mr. A T Rowlatt.) *Did you afterwards?*

(Third Officer Groves). *Well, what I took to be a reply. I saw what I took to be a light answering, and then I sent the word "What?" meaning to ask what ship she was. When I sent "What?" his light was flickering. I took up the glasses again and I came to the conclusion it could not have been a Morse lamp.*

(The Commissioner.) *Is the long and short of it this, that you did not get a reply, in your opinion?*

(Third Officer Groves). *In my opinion, no.*

London Inquiry Day 8

In the apparent absence of any other vessels in the area, the probability is that the ship they saw was in fact *Titanic*, though this was never established conclusively by the Inquiry. However, the timing of the various sightings, the vessel's appearance with extensive deck lighting, the rockets and the eventual disappearance of the vessel, all matched what had happened according to *Titanic's* timings to within a few minutes in each instance. The 'disappearance' could be explained as *Titanic's* sinking, though the most suspicious aspect of the evidence was that while *Californian's* official ship's log was produced at the Inquiry, the 'scrap log' had gone missing. This latter log was the document where navigational events were first noted down contemporaneously, the information being transferred to the official log at the end of the watch. This line of questioning by the Inquiry Board was interesting if only because it was not also used in regard to *Titanic's* logs.

The reason the identity of 'the other ship' could not be established conclusively during the hearing was most probably due to the evasive and contradictory answers give by Lord and his junior officers. Lord, who was adamant the ship they could see was not the *Titanic*, dismissed the rockets that were seen as irrelevant company communication signals, even though they were in a regular pattern of only white rockets, a typical distress pattern, whereas Captain Lord's officers, 2nd Officer Stone, 3rd Officer Groves and Apprentice Officer Gibson, seemed very reluctant to admit that they believed them to be distress signals, although Groves eventually admitted his belief that they were "most definitely distress signals". They seemed to have been torn between two loyalties – telling the truth and what their Captain wanted them to say.

(The Commissioner.) *Speaking as an experienced seaman and knowing what you do know now, do you think that steamer that you know was throwing up rockets, and that you say was a passenger steamer, was the "Titanic"?*

(3rd Officer Groves) *Do I think it?*

Yes

(3rd Officer Groves) *From what I have heard subsequently?*

Yes

(3rd Officer Groves) *Most decidedly I do, but I do not put myself as being an experienced man.*

(The Commissioner). *But that is your opinion as far as your experience goes?*

- Yes, it is my Lord.

London Inquiry Day 8

Interestingly, SS *Californian's* position was recorded in the official log as being 30 nautical miles from where *Titanic* sank, a distance over which a ship's lights and rockets would not normally be seen, though the Inquiry seemed to accept the distance as "between 4 and 7 nautical miles". However, *Californian's* official log is mentioned and discussed at great length at the London Inquiry (Day 8) in an effort by the Board to establish *Californian's* position at the time of the accident. The Chief Officer, 2nd Officer, 3rd Officer and Apprentice Officer were all grilled intensively to try to discover if there was any variation between the scrap log and the official log. Since the scrap log on this ship was normally discarded, page-by-page, there was no evidence of any discrepancy, and the matter remained unresolved.

Captain Lord was severely criticised for his lack of action and was subsequently sacked by Leyland Line, although he did obtain further command positions with other companies. The most significant part of the *Californian* story is that if she had been able to maintain contact either by Morse lamp or by wireless, the *Californian* would have steamed to the rescue and then again the outcome could have been very different. But the atmospheric conditions and *Californian's* Marconi operator Evans retiring for the night at 11.30 prevented this from happening.

However, while it is good to bear in mind that much of the safety at sea that we enjoy today comes directly from the *Titanic* disaster, there were two parts of the story that were neither mentioned nor discussed at either inquiry - *Titanic's* missing log and the attempt to steam for Halifax.

Fig 35. New York Inquiry with J Bruce Ismay (centre) and Senator Smith (4th from left) (Frances Wilson)

Fig 36. London Inquiry, Ismay on the stand and Chairman Lord Mersey at centre desk (R) (Frances Wilson)

CHAPTER 12
THE LEGACY

As a result of the two inquiries, several large international bodies responsible for the safety of ships at sea accepted the recommendations of the two inquiries into the *Titanic* disaster, which amounted to the following previously mentioned changes:

1. No speeding allowed through icefields

2. 24-hour wireless watch

3. Lifeboats enough for all on board, with no concessions for watertight compartments

4. US Coastguard Iceberg watch, which continues today

5. There was general agreement that signal rockets would henceforth only be used in the event of distress and no longer for inter-company communication at sea

The sinking of the *Titanic* has produced a huge rise in the level of safety for sea-going passengers. Every one of us knows that whether we are travelling on the Cross Channel ferry or a cruise ship to the Caribbean, there is a place in a lifeboat if required for each of us, and within a few hours of boarding such a cruise ship, there will be a lifeboat drill showing us exactly where that seat will be, and which crew members will be taking care of us.

The requirement for a 24-hour radio watch meant that ships with this facility would need at least two radio operators to cover this requirement. As already mentioned, the bodies concerned also agreed to standardize procedures and protocols, especially the fact there were two different Morse Codes in use, so as to improve safety and communications at sea.

The US Coastguard Iceberg Watch continues to this day. They visit the *Titanic* accident site every year on April 15th to lay a wreath in remembrance of the 1500 people who died in the disaster, and we should not forget that we owe our current safety standards at sea to their sacrifice.

FOR WHITE STAR:

As already mentioned, RMS *Olympic's* refit at the end of 1912 was extensive, and as one would expect, any problems with *Titanic's* design were examined closely by Harland & Wolff and acted on as necessary during this refit. *Olympic's* double bottom was extended up the sides of the central section to a level 6 feet above the waterline. 5 of the 15 watertight bulkheads were extended in height to level with the weather decks, and most important of all, she was fitted out with 64 lifeboats. The extension of the double bottom was primarily to improve the ships' watertight capability, and not to stiffen or strengthen the hull. It was also to prove useful for fuel oil storage when her furnaces were converted to oil-burning a few years later.

CHAPTER 13
THE CAPTAIN, ISMAY AND OTHERS

Over the last twenty years I have researched the *Titanic* story extensively, including the transcripts of the inquiries, newspaper reports and many books, and have come to the conclusion that there is much more to the story than some would have us believe. In particular, it seems Captain Smith had been unfairly criticised. He was of course the perfect scapegoat; he went down with his ship and so was unable to defend himself in the aftermath. His loyal officers and fellow captains did their best at the inquiries, but dramatic and often ridiculous speculation by the press proved more 'believable' than the truth that was often submerged, ignored or glossed-over. If there were any contradictions between the evidence, the court and the press tended to accept the more damaging or dramatic scenario.

Because his record as the most popular master on the Atlantic run (many regular White Star passengers would only travel if Smith was the Captain). He was known as the "Millionaires' Captain" as well as being the most highly-paid and experienced Atlantic sea captain of his time. However, he was quickly demoted at the Inquiries to being a hot-shot gung-ho commander who was more interested in his alleged dashing style of seamanship than the care and safety of his passengers. Both inquiries ruled that he had ignored the ice warnings received that day from other ships, and was steaming too fast for the conditions, while failing to post extra lookouts. But how can a man's reputation and career turn so drastically in a few disastrous hours? It may help to have a closer look at the man himself.

Edward John Smith was born in 1850 and brought up at 16 Well Street,

Hanley in Staffordshire. He left school at 13 years of age and four years later he went to sea to train as an officer in the Merchant Navy. He spent his first few years in square-rigged ships which gave him a first class grounding in all aspects of seamanship. By the age of 25 he had gained his Master Mariner's Certificate, and a year later he had his first command, the sailing ship *Lizzie Fennell* of the Gibson Line, trading mainly with South America. But he was enchanted by the beautiful White Star liners he had seen as a boy in Liverpool docks, and was determined that that was the direction he would go eventually. Then an opportunity arose at the age of 30 in 1880 and he signed on as 3rd officer on White Star's SS *Runic*, a difficult and courageous decision, stepping down from being a captain with 4 years seniority to a very junior officer rank. But White Star was the shipping line with which he was to spend the rest of his life, literally.

He married Eleanor in 1886 and the following year became 1st Officer on the White Star ship he first fell in love with as a boy, RMS *Britannic*. The step up from 3rd officer to 1st officer was huge (similar to going from a naval Sub Lieutenant to Lieutenant Commander) and demonstrated the high regard in which his employers now held him. Their daughter Helen Melville (known as Mel) was born in 1888, the same year he was given his first White Star command - RMS *Baltic*. Captain Smith continued as a White Star captain throughout his career commanding 18 of their passenger vessels, and by the turn of the century he was acknowledged as the Company's Commodore, carrying out the maiden voyages for all their new ships, including RMS *Olympic* in 1911, and of course, RMS *Titanic* in 1912.

Captain Smith had something of a reputation as an accident-prone commander, although there was only one accident in his early years as a captain. In January 1889 he ran SS *Republic* (3,700 tons) aground on Sandy Hook at the entrance to New York harbour, but floated off undamaged with the next tide. Nine years later, in May 1898, SS *Majestic* (10,000 tons) struck the quay at Liverpool causing minor damage to her bow plates. He ran aground again 11 years later with SS *Adriatic* (24,000 tons) outside

New York harbour in November 1909, and in 1911 at the end of her maiden voyage in June, he reversed RMS *Olympic* (52,000 tons) over a tug and almost sank it. In September that same year, *Olympic* collided with the *Hawke*, as described earlier.

One can see that as the size of ships grew so did the chances of an accident, but when the *Olympic* Class came along, they were the largest ships in the world, in fact the largest movable man-made objects of any kind, and everyone involved in their navigation and handling was on a very steep learning curve. Captain Smith and his pilot were occasionally caught out by the slower response and other effects of these enormously powerful and heavy leviathans.

It seems it was the sheer size of these ships that caused the difficulties, something the designers had not considered or allowed for. At that time it seems no one had thought that some extra training or practice might be a good idea; maybe everyone just assumed that these highly experienced and proficient officers would simply rise to the occasion without any difficulty.

Smith's penultimate accident happened as he and pilot Captain George Bowyer were taking *Titanic* out of her berth at the start of her maiden voyage from Southampton on April 10th. In spite of moving very slowly aided by tugs, it seems a little too much power was applied and the wash from *Titanic's* propellers strained and then broke the stern lines of the SS *New York* which was berthed just a few yards away on the outer wharf of the liner terminal, ahead of *Titanic*. As the *New York's* stern swung out towards *Titanic's* side, a quick-thinking tug master placed his vessel between the two ships and pulled the *New York* clear, avoiding a collision by a mere 4 feet. However, it was a curious accident to almost-happen; Smith and Bowyer together had docked and un-docked the *Olympic* from that same berth many times without incident. Perhaps the build-up of ships that cluttered up the port due to the coal strike had reduced the available space, making close-quarters incidents more likely.

I have not researched the subject in detail, but I suspect that Smith's accident record was no worse than any other captain of his time, bearing in mind that the shipping industry was still in the transition period from sail to steam, with all that that implies in terms of ship handling and steering orders and the literally massive increases in size.

In 1888 Smith joined the Royal Naval Reserve (RNR) with the rank of lieutenant; he retired from RNR in 1905 with the rank of Commander. His RNR commission allowed his ship to fly the blue ensign instead of the usual red ensign, provided he had sufficient RNR members among his crew, which he usually did.

In 1898 his ship SS *Majestic* was commandeered by the government as a transport ship during the Boer War. As an RNR officer he was a natural choice for such a task. The ship was painted white and with her new Service number, 62, stencilled on the sides. The ship's fine carpets were removed, but it is not known what other changes were made to equip *Majestic* for her new role. Smith carried out two successful voyages from Liverpool to Capetown and back and was awarded the Transport Medal (South Africa clasp) for his services. A little later in 1903 he was awarded the RNR Service Medal after 15 years service. In 1899 *Majestic* was returned to White Star passenger service. Captain Smith always wore his medals with great pride.

SPEED

(The Attorney-General.) *You have told me now what your answer is. What was your answer?*

(Ismay) *I should say if a man can see far enough to clear ice, he is perfectly justified in going full speed.*

(The Attorney-General.) *Then apparently you did not expect your Captain to slow down when he had ice reports?*

(Ismay) *No, certainly not.* London Inquiry Day 16

At the 36-day London inquiry, as mentioned earlier, several mail ship captains, including those of *Olympic* and *Carpathia*, stated they would probably have navigated their ships at the same speed as Smith did. Significantly, Chairman Lord Mersey said he could not blame Captain Smith for speeding through the icefields "*as he was only doing what other equally skilled men would do in the same position*". Ismay's evidence above supports this view and it was one of major disparities between the two inquiries.

The US Senate Sub Committee – the American inquiry - lasted for 18 days, starting 4 days after the disaster in the Waldorf Hotel in New York. It was moved to Washington half way through. In the report of the American inquiry Captain Smith was blamed for the accident due to "navigating his ship at too high a speed and for failing to post extra lookouts".

In the final US report, Smith was also criticised for not changing course at the usual point, ignoring wireless warnings of icebergs from other ships and failing to provide the lookouts with searchlights. I researched each of these criticisms and came up with the following conclusions:

"Navigated his ship at too high a speed" was the main outcome of the US inquiry, which placed full responsibility for those 1500 deaths firmly with Captain Smith. This was a statement with which Captain Smith would not and could not have disagreed; he was the Captain and was 100% responsible. But blame is another matter.

Captain Smith's reasons for maintaining his speed are several:

1. The ship had a schedule to keep and arriving late at an important destination did not look good for the shipping company in terms of publicity and reliability in a fiercely competitive market – the New York Atlantic run.

2. The myth that Ismay was pushing Smith to ever-increasing speeds 'so that they could create a sensation by arriving a day early' simply does

not stand up to scrutiny; to do so would have seriously inconvenienced the passengers and their waiting families and colleagues in terms of accommodation and travel disruption. In any event, speed was not White Star's obsession, unlike Cunard whose ships were 100 feet shorter and 8,250 GRT tons lighter than the *Olympic* class ships. White Star's marketing strategy was that their ships were designed for the highest standards of luxury and comfort, not outright speed. In addition, Ismay is on record as saying at the New York inquiry, *"I would neither criticise nor encourage my chauffeur nor my captain in matters of speed."*

3. Evidence was given at both inquiries that there was another reason for the daily increase in the ship's speed; this was her maiden voyage and all the new ship's systems had to be tested under actual operational conditions, as opposed to her single day's sea trials spent whizzing round the Irish sea to see how she handled, with no cargo or passengers. Once fully laden at sea though, the engineers tested her engines, gradually working up each day towards her designed top speed of 23 knots (though she never reached that point). Five of her 27 boilers were yet to be lit so she had some hither-to un-tapped power in reserve. Also to be tested were the ship's electrics, hydraulics, ventilation, refrigeration, bathroom facilities and water supply, communications and the ship's internal telephones and all the equipment in the galleys. Running in and 'working up' a new ship is a massive task for the entire crew, not just the officers on the bridge and in the engine room, constantly balancing the extra work load against the safe navigation of the ship. To assist in the 'work-up' process, *Titanic* had on board a team of 8 skilled experts known as the 'guarantee party', headed by Harland & Wolff's general manager and designer Thomas Andrews. This was, and still is, a normal part of any ship's maiden voyage, for obvious reasons. The group comprised fitters, electricians, marine engineers, telephone engineers, carpenters, etc. One member of *Titanic's* group was a 16-year old apprentice who had won his place on the voyage in a draw. None of the Guarantee Party survived.

Unbelievably, one system that remained untested was the lifeboats; there had been no lifeboat drill on *Titanic* during that fateful voyage. A drill was planned for the Sunday morning, the day she hit the berg, but it was postponed by the Captain in favour of a church service for the passengers. Two boats (the two 'emergency' boats, not proper lifeboats) had been lowered and launched in Southampton to demonstrate to the Board of Trade Inspector that the new Welin Davit system worked so that he could then sign off the ship as "fit to carry migrant passengers" (see the BoT report on Page 6). Only a dozen or so of the crew were involved on this occasion; but when they had to launch the lifeboats for real a few days later, most of the crew had little idea of how to go about it.

4. *Titanic* was designated "RMS *Titanic*" which meant that White Star had a contract with the British Royal Mail for *Titanic* to carry mail across the Atlantic. The company was paid well to do this but punctuality was essential and there were swingeing financial penalties for late delivery. If a Mail Ship arrived late at New York the company was fined a £1 and1 shilling (a guinea) per minute. In 1912 this worked out at £1,500 per day. In today's money (2019) that would have been £167,500. What captain would willingly put his employers, his ship and his career in that position? The ship had a large sorting office on board, manned by Royal Mail staff. They all died. Hundreds of thousands of items of mail went down with the ship and were never recovered.

5. The suggestion that the ship was going for the Blue Riband has already been dealt with and dismissed in Chapter 7. However, if there was anything competitive about *Titanic's* speed, it was probably to make a faster crossing than her slightly older sister ship, *Olympic*, whose best speed so far was 21.5 knots and *Titanic* had already beaten that.

6. It is easy to lose sight of the fact that Captain Smith and his contemporaries had all served their time 'before the mast' as young trainee officers in the beautiful tall sailing ships of that era. Consequently Smith had passed through icefields many, many times and understood

the dangers very well. One can only imagine how difficult it must have been navigating a sailing ship through such waters. Slower maybe than *Titanic*, but much more 'sluggish' on the helm, requiring huge amounts of skill, anticipation and concentration to navigate safely. Smith had all this experience behind him and one can imagine the enormous confidence he would have felt with *Titanic's* strength, power and speed literally right under his feet.

CHANGE OF COURSE (Fig 12)

At one point in the US inquiry, Captain Smith was criticised for not changing course as normal at "the Corner", a notional navigational point in the middle of the Northern Atlantic (42 degrees N, 47 degrees W) where ships would re-set their courses for the final leg into US ports on the east coast. The course from the Corner to New York was 266 degrees 'True'. By early afternoon on the day of the accident, Smith had already received 3 ice warnings from nearby ships and decided, after discussion with his officers, to take a more southerly course to avoid the ice, so he delayed his course change from 242 degrees to 266 degrees for 45 minutes, which set the ship on track for New York but some 10 nautical miles further south. The delayed change in course was part of Smith's plan to negotiate the ice safely, and was discussed and planned in detail with his officers. It certainly was not careless navigation!

EXTRA LOOKOUTS

Both the Inquiries insisted that the Captain should have posted extra lookouts that night, knowing, as he clearly did, that he was approaching the ice fields. The most obvious additional position, in their view, was at the stemhead of the ship. However, this may not have helped for the following reasons: (see Fig 37)

It is true that the stem head was 100 feet forward of the fore mast, but it was only 53 feet above the waterline. On the other hand, the crow's nest was 89 feet above the waterline. These two heights give elevated visual distances to the horizon of 8.9 nm and 11.6 nm respectively, a difference of 2.7 nm. Which means that at 22 knots any visible object could, in theory, be seen 7 minutes and 20 seconds sooner from the crow's nest in spite of it being 100 feet further aft. As a sea-going navigator, Captain Smith would have known this. We must also bear in mind that there were at least three officers and an assistant quartermaster on the bridge, giving a total of 6 pairs of eyes all searching for any danger ahead. Note that Quartermaster Hichens on the wheel had no forward or outside view at night as the dimly-lit wheelhouse was curtained-off from the bridge so as not to affect the bridge officers' night vision. Hichens would have been concentrating totally on steering the ship's course as accurately as possible, a difficult task at the best of times and calling for considerable skill.

Ironically, experts date the ice of that berg as being over 3,000 years old, yet it was probably less than a month from melting away!

J BRUCE ISMAY (Fig 6)

J Bruce Ismay was an enigmatic character. He was a key figure in the tragedy although dismissing any suggestion this was so. He was born into a wealthy Liverpool family with a loving mother and an austere father. Educated at Harrow he was a very unhappy schoolboy, but nevertheless, was clearly brought up to be a gentleman. Having gone into shipping in his twenties, he eventually became a director and then chairman of the American company International Mercantile Marine, having sold White Star to IMM earlier. Therefore, as the Managing Director of White Star, he was also the main shareholder in the company that owned *Titanic* and of 150 other White Star ships. He was adamant that he was travelling on *Titanic's* maiden voyage as a passenger (although a non-paying passenger) simply out of interest with no intention of controlling or managing any aspects of the maiden voyage.

However, the story seems to suggest that he may have had some input before the accident by discussing possible speed changes over the next few days, not with Captain Smith, but with Chief Engineer Bell. He gave evidence at the New York inquiry to this effect. He was interested primarily in the engineering aspects of 'running in' the ship's massive engines prior to discussing them later with the Captain.

After the collision with the iceberg there is strong evidence that Ismay and Captain Smith discussed the idea of taking the ship to Halifax, (see Chapter 9) at which point Smith ceased to be 'God' in his own ship but simply Ismay's employee, for he seems to have agreed, however reluctantly, with Ismay's half-baked suggestion, even before either of them knew the full extent of the damage to the ship's hull. Smith gave the order "Slow Ahead" without fully realizing how mortally wounded his ship was. However, it seems strange that this was never disclosed or discussed at either inquiry. It was such a crucial link in the tragic chain of events that cost 1500 lives, and would have been a gift to those who wished to pillory Smith as well as Ismay. Yet somehow it never happened.

Ismay had two adversaries in New York; Senator Smith, chairman of the US Senate Sub-committee, and the press. Both these groups had decided that Ismay should not have survived by taking a place in a lifeboat when there were hundreds of passengers still on board and doomed to die in the sinking. They saw Captain Smith as having taken the honorable decision to go down with his ship, and seemed to believe for some extraordinary reason that the White Star's Chairman should have done the same.

There is little logic to this view; if we were to compare this accident with a hire car crash, then it is absolutely clear that the driver is responsible or to blame, not the owner of the hire car company, even if he or she happened to be travelling in that car at the time. But it did present a wonderful opportunity to sell lots of newspapers to the horrified readers. It also fitted in well with the American public's view of "guilty by press reporting". We must also be aware that several *Titanic* authors and commentators agree that the results of both inquiries were pre-determined before the hearings started, and that any evidence that supported their view was happily received, while any evidence which contradicted their intended findings was either ignored or dismissed.

With Ismay's own testimony in mind, imagine if you can standing on that sloping deck with sea water washing round your feet and a half empty lifeboat a few feet away. No sign of women or children on that part of the deck and yet the sight of other men being ordered into the lifeboat by the ship's officers. It was, from most reports, almost the last lifeboat to leave the doomed ship and Captain Smith himself, according to one witness, was ordering you to get in the boat. There seems to be no logic in allowing a partially empty boat to sail away while you just stand and watch, knowing that was your last chance to avoid a cold and ghastly death – a very peculiar kind of suicide. Perhaps most of us would do the same as Ismay did. And yet Ismay was labelled a coward, a destroyed man at 50 as a result of giving in to that most basic of all human instincts, survival.

H G Wells wrote in the *Daily Mail* at the time *"By the supreme artistry of chance it fell to the lot of that tragic and unhappy gentleman to be aboard and to be caught by the urgent vacancy in the (life) boat and the snare of the moment. Let no untried man say he would have behaved better in his place."*

Apart from Ismay's own description of the events of that terrible evening, there were numerous other reports of how Ismay ended up in that lifeboat; Captain Smith was mentioned by at least one witness as ordering him into the boat and so was Chief Officer Wilde and at least one other un-named officer. Some witnesses say the deck was crowded with desperate folk hoping to get a place in a boat, while other reports agree with Ismay – that part of the boat deck was clear with absolutely no women or children in sight. Two women described how Ismay assisted them into a departing lifeboat, thereby saving their lives. At this time, men were also being ordered into the boats, another factor that might have persuaded Ismay to take that fateful step. Clearly he had two choices; step into the boat and risk the attack on his reputation from the press, or stay where he was and die. Since he was not preventing anyone, especially a woman or child, from having that seat (the boat was only partially loaded) then the charge of cowardice should not have been an issue.

The mixed and varied descriptions of what happened may possibly be explained by the fact it was night time and it would have been difficult to recognise or remember any particular person easily. As Ismay's lifeboat was occupied mainly by Lebanese steerage passengers, not many of them would know who he was anyway. Other boat deck accounts may be the result of mistaken identities. For example, there was one report of Captain Smith being seen in the water, handing a small child up into a lifeboat before swimming away to his death; all very unlikely, we now know.

2ND OFFICER LIGHTOLLER (Fig 4)

Charles Lightoller, *Titanic's* 2nd Officer, has been mentioned elsewhere. He went to sea as a cadet at the age of 13 and served his time on various tall sailing ships, gaining his First Mate's ticket in 1898. He left the Merchant Navy for a while and became a gold prospector In Canada. When this venture failed he became a cowboy, a hobo and a cattle wrangler in cattle ships. He joined White Star in 1900 as Fourth Officer on the SS *Medic*, serving on most of White Star's vessels, eventually as a senior officer but never held a command.

He was the most senior officer to survive the *Titanic* disaster and obviously felt it his responsibility at the inquiries to defend to the best of his ability his shipmates, his Captain, the crew and his employers. He even tried to defend the Board of Trade. In the witness box he could be a little belligerent but often very witty, probably due to the indignation felt by the entire British crew at the American authorities' high-handed decision to hold a US Senate Inquiry and locking them up in a hotel, denying them any outside contact, including from their families at home. One small group did escape onto a UK-bound ship but were hauled back by the US Coastguard before the ship left the harbour.

Lightoller's wit was probably very much enjoyed by those who were critical of the sub-committee's Chairman, Senator Smith, whose lack of knowledge of the sea should have rendered him totally unqualified to conduct such an important inquiry. Lightoller would also have been seriously irritated by the pompous attempts at showing off the verbal skills of the American assessors and lawyers – all total landlubbers to a man.

In his efforts to defend his colleagues, Lightoller was a little disingenuous occasionally, and described the weather conditions as 'all set against us' when there was no wind and a glassy surface to the sea. He later admitted 'using the whitewash brush' to avoid the pitfalls of some of the very aggressive questioning that was attempting to place blame for the tragedy on anyone foolish enough to cave in. It was clear that the US Senate Sub-committee was less interested in what went wrong than simply finding someone to blame, and that they had already decided who that would be – Captain Smith and his officers (maybe plus a few others).

Lightoller served with distinction in WW1 as a destroyer captain, and was awarded the DSC and bar for his courageous actions. He also 'served' during WW2 when he and his son took their family motor yacht *Sundowner* on several trips to Dunkirk and recovered 127 of our soldiers. The yacht is on display at the Maritime Museum in Ramsgate.

QUARTERMASTER ROBERT HICHENS (Fig 11)

Robert Hichens was 30 years old and lived in Southampton at the time of sinking, although he was born in Aberdeen. He had previously lived in Devon, where he had married and started his own family in 1906. He worked as a fisherman in Newlyn but then joined the Royal Navy Reserve and trained in all aspects of seamanship, eventually becoming a Quartermaster and gaining his Master Mariner's certificate. He hoped one day he might become an officer. Then realizing that work for seamen was scarce in the West Country, he moved his family to Southampton and obtained work with British India Lines and Union Castle.

Since February 1912, most of the country's merchant fleet was laid up for lack of coal due to a miners' strike. Just as the strike was beginning to bite and poverty loomed for most of Southampton's sea faring folk Robert Hichens obtained work as a quartermaster with White Star for the RMS *Titanic's* maiden voyage.

He was a stocky man of 5ft 6ins, allegedly with a disagreeable personality, and was severely criticised by his passengers in lifeboat No 6 for using foul language and refusing to go back to the site of the sinking to pick up survivors (he called them 'the stiffs') in the water. First class millionaire passenger 'Molly' Brown threatened to throw him out of the boat after taking charge and encouraging the passengers to row to keep warm, much to Hichens' dislike. He served on a small ship in the Army Service Corps during WW1 and later moved to Devon, where he was jailed for 5 years for the attempted murder of his former business partner.

It has been alleged by Lady Louise Patten (Lightoller's granddaughter) that at the moment of the accident, Hichens, on the wheel, turned it the wrong way. Although there is circumstantial evidence to support this, it was denied at the inquiry by 6th Officer Moody who was stationed at the wheel to confirm that all helm orders were carried out correctly. Yet another contradiction in this complicated story.

Fig 37. Model showing the relationship between the crow's nest and the stemhead (Author)

CHAPTER 14
NEMESIS

From my research of the transcripts of the inquiries, I have discovered a new side to Captain Smith's character, a side that was largely ignored by the Inquiry's Board members although many of the witnesses gave evidence to support Captain Smith as strongly as possible.

This next section is a supposed dialogue showing how Smith would have defended his position in court, if he had survived. The words are based on what various witnesses said about Captain Smith and his recorded actions during the last few hours of his, and his ship's, life. Information was also acquired from G C Coopers' book "*Titanic* Captain". This is how I think Smith would have given his evidence to the Inquiry Board:

2055: After the Widener's dinner party, I returned to bridge; discussed temperature, no wind and clear viz with Lightoller. Also that reflected light would show icebergs at about 2 miles range. *"If haze develops we will have to slow down"*

2120: I went to my cabin flat and said to Lightoller, *"If it becomes at all doubtful let me know at once. I shall be just inside".* Lightoller told 6th Officer Moody to warn the lookouts to watch for small ice and growlers.

2130: Critical Ice report from *Mesaba* to *Titanic* describing massive ice dead ahead of us: Phillips acknowledged, but with no MSG code it did not go to the Bridge; I had no opportunity to read it.

2200 – 2340: I stayed on and around the bridge area and chart room all watch with 1st Officer Murdoch, 4th Officer Boxhall and 6th Officer Moody plus the 2 Quartermasters on the bridge. I did NOT go to sleep as alleged in the press! I was far too busy:

Updating the positions on the charts

Discussing the 4 ice reports with officers and crucially -

Working out best route through the ice with them.

2341: Lookouts reported *"Iceberg right ahead"* over the bridge telephone. The chart room is abaft the bridge and the wheelhouse so I could not hear Murdoch's orders to Hichens. Then we struck. I came out of the chart room and asked Murdoch *"What have we struck?" "An iceberg"* he replied. *"I stopped and put the engines full astern. Tried to port around it but we hit it."*

I said *"Close all watertight doors"*; *"Watertight doors already closed, sir"*

"Did you ring the emergency warning bell for the doors?" *"Yes, sir"*

Lightoller appeared on the bridge in his pyjamas and bare feet. Ship's carpenter reported 7 feet of water in the firemen's accommodation compartment and rising.

1200: Asked Chief Engineer Bell for a damage report; *"not good news Ted, although she should stay afloat for a few hours".*

Went to Marconi Room - *"Stand by to send distress message but not till I tell you".* Then I went down to inspect damage for myself with Thomas Andrews; 5 compartments had been opened in the impact and there was already 14ft of water in the fo'c'sle.

Andrews said 1 to 1 and a half hours (actually 2 and a half)

1205: 'UNCOVER THE BOATS'

I knew that we had enough boats for only half of the souls on board; Also that there was apparently not enough time left (1.5 hrs I was told) to complete that operation at night.

I only had 66 seamen in the crew and that number would dwindle rapidly as the boats were launched and sent away with 2-3 crew in each boat;

once a boat was filled and swung out it could take 5-10 mins to manually lower each boat to the water. There was not enough time to get them all away so we partially filled the boats to get as many away as possible, as fast as possible. Only a dozen of the crew had done it before!

I ordered Chief Officer Wilde to call for *"All hands on deck!"* to assist in loading the boats; my plan was to get as many boats as possible away as soon as possible so that they could be ready to pick up survivors in the water after the ship had gone. I was still hoping a rescue ship might arrive in time to avoid this, but I was becoming increasingly concerned that this would not happen.

I also had to avoid panicking the passengers; a free-for-all or riot on the boat deck would be disastrous. I briefed my officers to give the impression to the passengers we were waiting for rescue and launching the lifeboats was a 'precaution' but Birkenhead rules still apply – *"Women and children first".*

I ordered 2 junior officers to get all the First Class passengers on deck and sent Murdoch to organize the stewards to do the same for the Second and Third Class passengers.

Released steam from the boilers via the boiler relief pipes on the 4 funnels was a deafening noise; it woke all the remaining passengers making the stewards' job easier but officers had difficulty communicating with each other and the crew.

1215: Asked Marconi operators to send CQD with our position 41.44N - 50.24W. I knew this position was incorrect but the CQD was more important. The position correction could come later. Replies came in within minutes; Only *Carpathia* was close enough to help - 58 nautical miles away. Apart from visiting the Marconi room, I remained on the bridge so my officers knew where to find me.

4th Officer Boxhall offered to check the dead-reckoning position and

I thanked him. He returned to the chart room and came out later with 41.46N - 50.14W. I told him to take this correction to the Marconi room for transmission.

1230: SWING OUT THE BOATS

Lightoller asked if he should start to swing out the boats and I said *"Yes, swing out, then start putting women and children into the boats".* Passengers were reluctant and fearful about entering the boats.

1240: Marconi operator Bride came to the bridge to tell me *"Carpathia" is on her way; ETA in 4 hours".* I went to the wireless room and spoke to Phillips. *"I am sending CQD"* he said. *"Try the new SOS"* quipped Bride, *"this may be your last chance to send it"* and we all laughed drily.

The band came on the deck to play. First boat away (#7) at 1240

1240 DISTRESS ROCKETS

Boxhall asked if he should send up distress rockets. I said *"Yes, send one up every 5 or 6 minutes."* I also told Boxhall to use the signal lamp to contact the steamer we could see a few miles away to the north. *"Tell him to come at once; we are sinking."*

0100: I gave orders for the ship's firearms to be handed out to senior officers. They were not needed immediately but could be useful later.

0115: The engineer officers stayed below in the engine room to keep the pumps running and the lights working on the boat deck, knowing they would almost certainly die, and they all did - 35 of them.

THE MUSICIANS STAYED and they all died too.

0200 – 0220: I saw a bunch of ship's crew sitting in a lifeboat and ordered them out, calling them 'damned cowards'. They climbed out and crept away shamefully and more passengers climbed in.

Boxhall had been working non-stop trying to contact that ship with the signal lamp, sending up rockets in between sessions. I ordered him into a lifeboat and passed his job over to QM Rowe. Still no readable response from the ship's Morse lamp, just mixed up flickering.

I tried to get some lifeboats to come back alongside to take people off from the gangway hatch, which was now at sea level, but none of them seemed to understand what I was saying.

I found Mrs Harris refusing to leave her husband and I told her to get into a lifeboat so that he has a chance to save himself. She did.

I went to the Marconi room to release the two operators who had worked constantly all evening. I told them *"Every man for himself; look after yourselves; I release you. That's the way of it at this kind of time."*

The end was near and I went to the bridge to wait; my steward Arthur Paintin appeared at my side, loyal to very end.

Footnote: *The failed attempt to sail for Halifax occurred around midnight and would most probably not have been mentioned by Captain Smith as he would have realized it had been a mistake. Halifax was not mentioned by anyone at either Inquiry.*

CHAPTER 15
DISCOVERY OF THE WRECK OF TITANIC

Fig 38. *Titanic's* bow section (Robert Ballard/Ken Marschall)

Fig 39. *Titanic's* stern section. The wreckage lies rotting away 12,500 feet below the surface. (Robert Ballard/Ken Marschall)

After almost 12 years of planning and searching, the wreck was discovered to be in two massive sections by a joint US/French team, headed by Professor Robert Ballard in 1985, using a submersible called *Alvin* (Fig 39). Not only fascinating in itself, the discovery threw up many significant clues regarding the disaster. However, the conspiracists noted that one of the propeller blades was stamped with the number 401, *Titanic's* build number, claiming this as evidence of the ships having been switched since one of *Titanic's* propeller blades was used to repair RMS *Olympic* in February 1912 following her accident while leaving New York. The reality was that this particular blade was fitted to *Titanic* anyway.

The question of exactly where and how extensive the hull damage was could not be established as that area of the hull was deeply embedded in the ocean floor. Almost 20 years later in 2003, another dive team lead by Richie Kohler and John Chatterton, discovered a third part of the ship 500 metres away (Fig 40 and 41), consisting of two 92-foot wide sections of the ship's double bottom, each containing about 30 feet of the keel, and established as being from the part of the hull immediately behind funnel No 3, which is exactly where she broke up. (Paintings and drawings of the wreck are by Ken Marschall, all based on hundreds of photos and hours of video footage).

Fig 40. Double bottom showing cleanly broken-off edges of the steel (B Matsen)

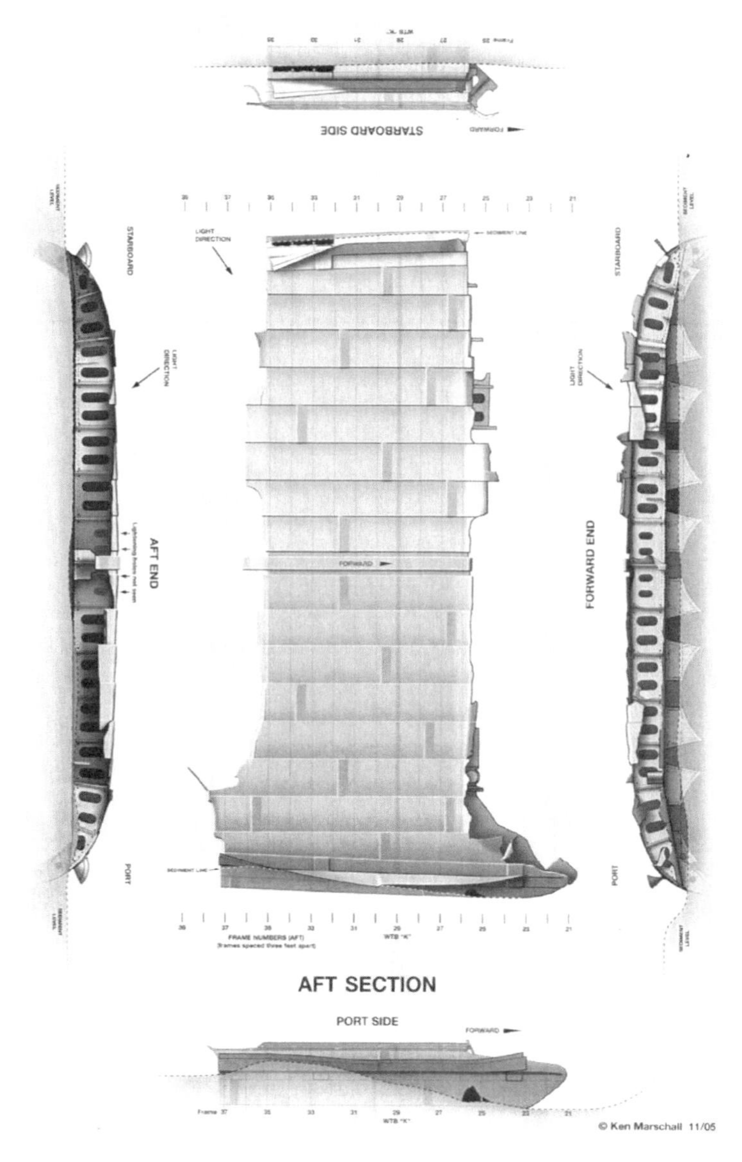

Fig 41. Drawing of the aft piece of hull (B Matsen)

The interesting feature of these images is the clean 'snapped-off' broken edges of the steel (Fig 40) strongly indicating that the ship's breakup was by 'sagging' as opposed to the popular view of her 'hogging'. This is because steel breaks off cleanly when under tension. Examination of the broken steel of the superstructure shows the typical explosive nature of a compression fracture.

Of course this is a huge contradiction to the accepted story of her 'hogging', reinforced by the various images shown in books and films. But this evidence supports the view if the sinking shown in Jack Thayer's contemporaneous sketches shown in Fig. 34. In spite of this new evidence, there is still strong resistance to the idea; the jury is still out.

EPILOGUE

During WW1 in July 1918, Lieutenant Commander Charles Lightoller RNR, in command of destroyer HMS *Garry*, was on convoy escort duty off the North Yorkshire coast when he attacked a U-Boat, UB-110, with depth charges. When she surfaced *Garry* rammed her and she sank immediately. 34 survivors were picked up. Lightoller's decision to ram the U-Boat was successful but left his ship with a severely damaged bow, and he would obviously need to return to his base on the Humber as soon as possible. Remembering what happened when *Titanic* tried to get to Halifax, Lightoller could see that steaming ahead would scoop up masses of seawater and possibly overwhelm his ship. As a result, he brought his ship home going astern all the way. He sent a signal saying "*Returning under own power stern first - 6 knots.*" He was awarded a bar to the DSO he had already been awarded for his courage and seamanship. If only Captain Smith had had the same thought.

COULD THE DISASTER HAVE BEEN PREVENTED?

We have looked at what happened and explained many of the reasons and outcomes; so what might have prevented the disaster? I found 5 areas that could have changed things enormously.

1. Enough lifeboats would have been a good start! Though even that may not have totally prevented loss of life as many people died from hypothermia in the lifeboats. Today we understand that proper training for the crew, together with a drill for the passengers, are essential to minimizing the effects of this kind of disaster. Other than a handful who had lowered the two emergency boats for the Board of Trade Inspector, *Titanic's* crew had had no experience of how to lower the lifeboats, and many, including some of the officers, believed a full load of passengers

would cause the launching gear to fail and tip them all in the sea! This was totally incorrect and a serious mistake born entirely out of a lack of training. The new Welin-designed davits and all the associated gear were specifically designed and tested to take the weight of a full lifeboat and to deliver it safely down to the sea.

Bearing in mind the icy waters the ship was to pass through, more and better equipment and stores in the lifeboats to provide warmth and sustenance for the lifeboats' passengers would also have helped. This of course would have required adequate systematic checking of the lifeboats and their equipment, which had not happened, in spite of Lightoller's glowing account of the ship's inspection by BoT Inspector Captain Maurice Clarke. After the sinking it was found that some lifeboats did not have a bailer or even a bung in the bottom, requiring the passengers to try to stop the boat flooding with their own clothing, leaving them with less clothing to keep warm and their feet in the freezing water for hours. Only one lifeboat was equipped with a mast and sail and many had no torch, compass, water or emergency food rations. But then the disastrously small number of lifeboats were on board merely to satisfy the regulations.

It may be true to say that even if *Titanic* had been provided with the originally-planned number of lifeboats (64), there probably would not have been enough time to load them all to capacity and to lower them, so that many passengers may have been left to swim for it in the hope of being picked up by a lifeboat. This may have been unlikely anyway, since in the event many of the crew and passengers refused to go back to pick up survivors for fear of being swamped or capsizing, yet another example of the lack of training for the crew.

(The Commissioner). *Then how long would it take you to get lifeboats No. 4 and No. 6 uncovered?*

(2nd Officer Lightoller). *Well, it would take us from 15 minutes to 20 minutes to uncover No. 4; then to coil the falls down, then to swing out and lower it down to A deck would take another six or seven minutes at least.*

London Inquiry Day 12

2. It is indisputable that *Titanic* should have stayed where she was after the accident; the ship was flooding but the pumps were almost holding, and she most probably could have stayed afloat until help arrived. The decision to set off for Halifax was a disastrous one that drastically shortened *Titanic's* time on the surface. The curious fact is that neither inquiry made use of this part of the story even though it seemed their main object was to discredit Captain Smith, for it would seem the attempt to steam for Halifax was Smith's only real mistake.

3. If the ship had been going more slowly, there is no doubt there would have been even more time for the officers on the bridge to respond to the lookouts' report. But we have looked at the reasons why she was going at such a speed and, I believe, explained them satisfactorily. Maybe some responsibility lies with Royal Mail for penalizing Mail Ships so drastically for not arriving on time. It is difficult for us not to view this with our 21st century eyes, but it must be seen in the context of maritime practice at the time as presented by the four Mail Ship captains who gave their evidence to the London Inquiry, a view which was supported by the Chairman himself.

4. Wireless messages received by the ship and requiring the Captain's attention all had the code 'MSG' preceding the time/date code. As mentioned earlier, this stands for 'Master's Special Gram' and the message was therefore required to be taken to the bridge by the Marconi operator, read and signed for by the Captain (or Officer of the Watch), placed on the bridge noticeboard for the other officers to see, and then acknowledged

by wireless message to the sender. The interest in the ice-message from Baltic that found its way into Ismay's pocket was a complete red herring; yes, it was unusual, perhaps improper, but it had no connection with the outcome.

5. As we have seen, two of the key wireless messages warning of ice dead ahead did not have the MSG code and therefore were not sent to the bridge. If they had been seen by the Captain, then most probably his response would have been different. Maybe he would have ordered a reduction in speed and maybe that would have made a difference. It may be appropriate to look at Jack Phillips' response to those two non-MSG messages. Phillips was under a lot of pressure dealing with a backlog of passengers' messages, and maybe just for a moment he lost sight of the fact that messages that could possibly affect the navigation of the ship should, indeed must, take precedence over social or commercial messages from passengers, whether or not those messages had the necessary MSG prefix.

There are a lot of 'maybes' in there but my feeling is that Captain Smith, who had sailed through the same North Atlantic icefields scores of times, was well aware they were entering a potentially dangerous area, would have slowed right down if he had known that that group of icebergs was there, dead ahead. We just do not know for certain, but common sense and the huge benefits of hindsight tell us that the outcome would almost certainly have been very different.

REMARKABLE SURVIVALS

During the US Inquiry, Charles Lightoller was asked for his experiences as the ship was sinking. He explained that he was on the fast-disappearing boat deck helping to get the collapsible lifeboats away when a huge air intake for the ventilation system became submerged by a wave that swept him off his feet and the tons of water flowing down the ventilation shaft pinned him down onto the grill of the intake. There he remained for some time as the ship sank. He was lying on a rather flimsy grating, which, if it had collapsed would have dropped him 100 feet into the bowels of the ship. He said *"I was beginning to lose interest in the whole affair when there was a huge explosion deep down in the ship – a boiler perhaps – which shot me back up to the surface like a cork out of a bottle."* He then managed to swim and clamber onto the upturned collapsible lifeboat B and remained there until he was rescued at dawn, along with 30 other people who had also been hanging on.

One of the most remarkable survival stories was told by stewardess Violet Jessop. (Fig 10a). In 1911 she was on board RMS *Olympic* when the ship was in collision with HMS *Hawke*. She was uninjured in this incident, as were all the other passengers and crew. She was on board *Titanic* when she struck the iceberg in April 1912 and was fortunate enough to survive the sinking, having been ordered into lifeboat No 16 to act as a 'behaviour role model' for some of the migrant passengers who did not speak English. Sadly, her brother Frank, who was a member of the crew, did not survive (Fig 10b). Four years later in 1916 Violet was a VAD nurse on board HMHS *Britannic*, White Star's third *Olympic* Class ship which was then serving as a WW1 hospital ship (Fig 43). The *Britannic* struck a mine off the Greek coast on her way to the Dardanelles and Gallipoli. She went down in 55 minutes because all the windows and portholes on the lower decks were open due to the hot and humid climate and the lack, in those days, of proper air conditioning. The ship was empty except for the ship's company and medical staff (over 1000 people) as she was on her way out to pick up wounded from the war zone.

As *Britannic* was sinking, Violet was put into a lifeboat by an officer, even though the order to launch lifeboats had not yet been issued from the bridge; in fact the engine room had not been told "stop all engines" and the propellers were still turning! The stern was well out of the water with the propellers only partly submerged when several lifeboats were launched and then pulled into the propellers' wash and chopped to pieces, killing most of the occupants. Violet's lifeboat suffered the same fate, but by jumping out of the lifeboat in the nick of time, Violet survived with little more than a bump on the head. It would seem the lessons of four years earlier had not been fully learned, and that lifeboat training and drill were still not properly in place. 30 men were lost in the sinking, with only 5 bodies recovered for burial. Violet became known as "Miss Unsinkable".

WAS CAPTAIN SMITH TO BLAME FOR THE DISASTER?

Clearly, he made mistakes such as steaming for Halifax without waiting for the damage reports, then he ordered the lifeboats to be launched and loaded without proper instructions to his officers and crew, while knowing that there were insufficient places for those on board – a mere 50%.

But the background to all this was not Smith's fault; he was neither responsible nor to blame for the lack of the crew's emergency training or the shortage of lifeboats. That would all have been down to company decisions on their rules and regulations at sea by the White Star board, and they failed miserably. It seemed that the attention from White Star and IMM was focused more on selling tickets to passengers than it was on those passengers' safety.

ICE IN THE RIGGING

Probably another red herring, and certainly nothing to do with the sinking, but a lot of people got very excited about reports of passengers playing football with chunks of ice on the decks following the collision with the iceberg. It was thought by some that the ice was a result of the impact of *Titanic* striking the iceberg, sending shards of ice from the iceberg down onto the decks. I see this as fanciful nonsense as well as irrelevant, for these reasons:

Titanic's puny 50,000 ton impact was not likely to have any physical or structural effect on an iceberg that probably weighed several million tons! In any case, there was no violent sideways swipe against the ice. If there had been, then every person on board the ship would have known about it, but many were completely unaware. The most likely reason for the ice on the deck was that the impact, mild though it seemed to some, had actually loosened some of the ice that had accrued in the ship's overhead rigging due to the high humidity and the very low air temperature. Anyone who sailed in the North Atlantic or Russian convoys in WW2 will attest to that phenomenon.

THE SEEDS OF DISASTER - THE PERFECT STORM

Which of these contributing factors to the disaster can be described as Captain Smith's fault?:

1. Insufficient number of lifeboats:

The inadequate number of lifeboats would have been a White Star/H&W board room decision; they were never considered a good idea anyway since they 'sent out the wrong message' about how safe *Titanic* was. This approach to lifeboats was generally evident with all the other major shipping lines, not just *Titanic* and White Star.

2. Ineffective use of wireless:

As already mentioned, the use of wireless at sea and the growth of the Marconi company were relatively new factors and the industry had not yet worked out how best to make use of the new technology. Maybe Marconi himself was clear about how to use it, but commercial pressures from the companies involved seem to have failed to recognize the significance of this service and had watered down his original vision. The Marconi operators at that time were not ship's officers, but sub-contracted Marconi employees providing a wireless service at sea. There was always a tendency to prioritize messages according to their commercial value to the Marconi company, even though messages relating to navigation were required to go straight to the bridge. This did not always happen, as we now know, and Captain Smith would have had little control over how Philips and Bride ran their own 'business' other than to make the need and the request clear. With the relaxed approach to wireless at that time, *Californian's* Marconi operator Evans was acting normally when he went to his cabin 10 minutes before *Titanic* struck. If he had stayed on watch he would have heard *Titanic's* distress calls and maybe all would have been well.

3. Pressure on the Captain:

From the beginning, there have been stories about J Bruce Ismay pressuring Captain Smith to increase the ship's speed each day. There is no evidence for this other than in the press reports at the time. In fact Ismay stated in evidence that he would never interfere even with his own chauffeur's 'navigation' let alone his captain's! It is clear that any increase in the ship's speed was necessitated by the need to 'run in' the engines etc. There was also the considerable pressure from the Royal Mail contract to keep to schedule.

It seems the only occasion that Smith gave into any pressure from Ismay was when he agreed to try to steam the ship away to Halifax. But then he was to some extent bound by the fact Ismay was the Company Chairman and that he, Smith, was merely his employee.

4. Not enough lookouts:

In these conditions one can never have enough lookouts! However, there were two people in the crow's nest, 85 feet above the waterline, and four more on the bridge. If the conditions had been hazy then an extra lookout in the stem-head might have been a good idea, but there is no certainty that would have changed anything. Lookouts Fleet and Lee in the crow's nest did a great job seeing the iceberg when they did, but in terms of avoiding it, the biggest problem was the time taken for *Titanic* to respond to Murdoch's helm order, 'Hard a' starboard'!

5. Halifax:

The decision to make for Halifax was a disastrous one and one that must have shortened *Titanic's* life on the surface by a significant factor. If Smith had resisted Ismay's suggestion for 10 more minutes until he had received the damage reports from Bell, Andrews and the ship's carpenter, he would almost certainly never have moved the ship and she could have still been afloat when the *Carpathia* arrived at dawn.

6. The weather:

As already mentioned, the atmospheric and meteorological conditions were unusual; no wind with a glassy smooth sea, very cold and a temperature inversion that caused certain flickering visual effects that also seemed to reduce one's estimation of distances, as well as completely destroy any attempt at Morse Code communication by lamp. None of which was Smith's responsibility.

Footnote: *A temperature inversion is caused when a layer of warm air is trapped and compressed by a mass of colder air above it. This increases the density of the warm air, producing a lens-like quality that will bend light in an arc slightly greater than the earth's curvature such that there is a mirage type of effect. This makes objects look much closer than they really are and renders the estimation of distance very difficult. It probably accounts for the Californian's officers believing that they were much closer to Titanic than they were – estimated 7 nm as opposed to the actual 21 nm. These conditions are common in the North Atlantic at the point where extremely cold glacial air mixes with the warmer Gulf Stream air.*

Fig 42. HMTS *Olympic* spent WW1 as a troop transport ship.
(Peter Thresh)

RMS *Olympic* acted as a troop transport ship during WW1, and was immensely popular with the troops due to her comforts and spaciousness. She reverted to normal passenger service in 1920 and she continued as a passenger liner until sold in 1935 by her new owners Cunard, who had bought out White Star in 1934. She was scrapped in 1937.

The third ship in the Class, SS *Britannic*, never saw passenger service. By the time she was completed, WW1 had started and the demand for the Atlantic passenger service had melted away. She was moth-balled for over a year and eventually commandeered by the War Office and converted to a hospital ship as HMHS *Britannic* (Fig 43).

Fig 43. HMHS *Britannic*, sunk by a German mine in 1916 off the coast of Greece (Internet)

TO SUMMARISE

- *Titanic* was NOT weak; in fact she was much stronger than the regulatory requirements of the day.
- *Titanic* was built with the highest quality of steel and other materials.
- *Titanic's* speed was matched to the operational requirements of the ship.
- Despite what the Inquiries said, no one person was to blame, especially not Captain Smith.
- The accident was due to a cruel mix of complacency on the part of the owners and builders and an extraordinary combination of bad luck.
- The Conspiracy Theory is just that - a conspiracy with no real evidence to support it.
- There had been virtually no serious iceberg collisions in the North Atlantic in the previous 20 years and the type of collision that *Titanic* suffered was completely unknown.
- The subsequent changes to *Olympic* were a natural process of industrial improvement and development and not a criticism of *Titanic*.
- There is no certainty that a full complement of 64 lifeboats would have saved many more lives; there would have been insufficient time to load them all.
- Whatever happened to *Titanic's* Navigational log?

Bibliography:

"THE RIDDLE OF THE *TITANIC*"	Robin Gardiner and Dan van der Vat
"TITANIC – THE SHIP THAT NEVER SANK"	Robin Gardiner
"TITANIC IN PICTURE POSTCARDS"	Robert McDougall and Robin Gardiner
"A NIGHT TO REMEMBER"	Walter Lord
"DISCOVERY OF THE *TITANIC*"	Robert Ballard
"LAST LOG OF THE *TITANIC*"	David G Brown
"OLYMPIC AND *TITANIC* the truth behind the conspiracy"	Steve Hall and Bruce Beveridge
"TITANIC'S LAST SECRETS"	Brad Matsen
"HOW TO SURVIVE THE *TITANIC* – or the sinking of J Bruce Ismay"	Frances Wilson
"TITANIC CAPTAIN"	G J Cooper
"TITANIC and Other Ships"	Cdr. Charles H Lightoller RNR
"TITANIC AND LIVERPOOL"	Alan Scarth
"TITANIC"	Anton Gill
"THE MAN WHO SANK THE *TITANIC*"	Sally Nilsson
"THE STING OF THE *HAWKE*"	Samuel Halpern and Mark Chirnside
"TITANIC – HAYNES OWNERS MANUAL"	Richard de Kerbrech and David Hutchings
"*TITANIC*"	Peter Thresh
INTERNET	www.titanicinquiry.org

Acknowledgements:

They say that everyone has a book inside them and I discovered mine very late in life! I started to write this book whilst 'laid up' for medical reasons for almost a year as a means of saving my sanity. However, I would not have got this far without the help and support of a number of wonderful people:

My friend, Captain John Board, Master Mariner and the only person I know who has sailed in a Cunard/White Star ship – the third ship named Britannic - as a junior officer in the 1950s, has been most helpful with suggestions on *Titanic's* construction and layout. It was John who started me on this fascinating journey nearly 20 years ago.

My eldest son Christian, Fellow of the Royal Institution of Naval Architects (FRINA) and President of the RINA New Zealand Division, has been fulsome in his encouragement and guidance.

International *Titanic* historian and author Bruce Beveridge has devoted a huge amount of time to the manuscript, guiding me firmly and clearly on such mysteries as the use of italics for ships' names as well as helping me understand which of the many issues in *Titanic's* story are worthy of mention and which should be destined for the trash bin.

Maritime author and *Titanic* authority, Richard de Kerbrech MRINA, also helped me with some of the trickier details of *Titanic's* construction, partly through his book "*TITANIC* - the Haynes Owner's Workshop Manual".

Locally, I have received great encouragement and detail help with the manuscript from local historian, the late John Woodford (including a large number of postcards and photographs from his private collection), diver and ex-Lifeboat coxswain Martin Woodward MBE and my long-standing friends Peter Dalby and Don Webber BA (Hons). I am particularly grateful to another great friend, historian and author Ken Hicks MBE, FRSA, (Hon) FHA for his tireless and invaluable help with the proof readings needed to get this book published.

I extend my heartfelt gratitude to all these people. Thank you